EASY COMPANY SOLDIER

THE LEGENDARY BATTLES OF
A SERGEANT FROM WORLD WAR II'S
"BAND OF BROTHERS"

Sgt. Don Malarkey

WITH BOB WELCH

 ST. MARTIN'S GRIFFIN ◢◢ NEW YORK

www.stmartins.com

The Library of Congress has catalogued the hardcover edition as follows:

Malarkey, Don, 1921–
    Easy Company soldier : the legendary battles of a sergeant from World War II's "Band of Brothers" / Don Malarkey and Bob Welch.—1st ed.
        p. cm.
    ISBN-13: 978-0-312-37849-3
    ISBN-10: 0-312-37849-1
    1. Malarkey, Don, 1921– 2. United States. Army. Parachute Infantry Regiment, 506th. Company E. 3. World War, 1939–1945—Regimental histories—United States. 4. United Sates. Army—Parachute troops—History. 5. World War, 1939–1945—Campaigns—Western Front. 6. World War, 1939–1945—Personal narratives, American. 7. Soldiers—United States—Biography. I. Welch, Bob, 1945– II. Title.

D769.348 506th .M35 2008
940.54'1273092—dc22
[B]

2008004742

ISBN-13: 978-0-312-56323-3 (pbk.)
ISBN-10: 0-312-56323-X (pbk.)

10 9 8 7 6 5 4 3

Praise for *Easy Company Soldier*

"First of all, you're going to love this book. Mortar Sgt., second platoon, Don Malarkey . . . together, we were the best (not bragging). In training and in combat, we never had any problems. We've been friends for life, more than sixty-five years. He's my hero."
—William "Wild Bill" Guarnere, member of Easy Company and coauthor of the *New York Times* bestseller *Brothers in Battle, Best of Friends*

"Don Malarkey: an outstanding soldier in combat, a gentleman with the memory of an elephant who I will always consider to be an esteemed friend."
—Maj. Dick Winters, Commander, Easy Company and coauthor of the *New York Times* bestseller *Beyond Band of Brothers*

"Don Malarkey is a staunch patriot who truly understands the principles for which we fought. He contributed his all in building the reputation of the 101st Airborne as a great fighting unit. His life today epitomizes the standards which all good Americans should strive to emulate."   —Lt. Lynn "Buck" Compton, member of Easy Company and author of *Call of Duty*

"The graphic story of [Malarkey's] bloody fight from the shores of France to the heartland of Germany makes for fascinating reading and is an important chapter in our military history." —*Tucson Citizen*

"A poignant account of E Company's sacrifice and courage amidst the horror of war."   —*AmericanHeritage.com*

"Malarkey's story is an interesting combination of the chaos of war, his attachment to paramours and friends, and the consistent theme of his inner life. Readers who have enjoyed other installments in the history of the 101st Airborne will find this addition worthwhile."
—*America in WWII* magazine

"A dramatic profile of a tough, compassionate man . . . *Easy Company Soldier* is the story of battles and friendships, following orders and coming under fire. It is about the psychological and emotional toll of war. Meet Don Malarkey, and better understand every soldier who comes home."   —*The Sunday Oregonian*

TO IRENE, my wife and best friend of nearly sixty years; I miss you dearly, my darling. To my son, Michael, for listening to my stories over these many years and encouraging me to write this book. And to my three daughters, Martha, Sharon, and Marianne. You have loved an old fuddy-duddy of a dad who was sometimes insensitive to your needs. I love you all.

CONTENTS

EASY
COMPANY
SOLDIER

1

THE CHOICE

Bastogne, Belgium
January 3, 1945

One shot.

That's all it would take, I figured, as I warmed my hands around the campfire with a few other shivering soldiers. One shot and this frozen hell of Belgium's Ardennes Forest would be over for me.

It was January 1945, seven months since me and the guys in the 101st Airborne's 506th Parachute Infantry Regiment had jumped into that dark sky over Normandy. Now, a handful of us E Company guys were numb from war, death, and bitter cold and snow. In the flames' flickering light, I looked down at my boots, wrapped in burlap bags and purposely dipped in water so they'd freeze and keep my feet warmer.

One shot and those damn feet would never be cold again. One shot and the sight of Joe Toye and Bill Guarnere lying in the snow, each missing a leg, would never haunt me again.

Why Toye? Why not the SOB who I'd seen a few days ago slicing fingers off the dead German soldiers to get their rings, the guy who was almost smiling when he told me "cuttin' those fingers was just like cuttin' a candle in half." Toye was wounded in Normandy, Holland, and once here, coming back with his arm in a sling to fight. Maybe I'm biased because, like me, Joe was Irish, but hadn't he already paid the war piper?

And why Guarnere? He gets it trying to save Joe. The Germans are raining down artillery shells like a Fourth of July show gone wrong, and Bill sees Joe out there trying to get up and so runs across the snow to save his buddy. Sort of like one swimmer trying to help another swimmer who's drowning. And, boom, both end up drowning. At least it hadn't been Skip Muck, whose 1st Platoon was a few hundred yards away from our 2nd. He was closer than a brother to me.

I blew on my cupped hands to warm them up. I then put my right hand onto the pistol's holster, and around the wooden grip, cold as a frozen salmon. We were virtually surrounded by the Germans, the proverbial hole in the doughnut. And had been here for more than two weeks, though time wasn't easy to keep track of when you couldn't see beyond the fog and snow of some iceboxed forest that's so far from home that you can hardly remember what home is like anymore.

Sometimes, in the night, when the quiet wasn't feared as much, I would remember home. Not so much my family or our house in Astoria, where I'd grown up near where the Columbia River meets up with the Pacific Ocean, but the cabin.

It was snug to the Nehalem River, in Oregon's Coast Range. I lived like an Indian. Swam in the Nehalem each day. Dove for crawdads. Went bird hunting with a bow, carved from a yew tree. While crouched in a foxhole in Bastogne, I remembered watching the riffle in the river, knowing that beneath that water lived sea-run cutthroat trout and crawdads galore. I remembered easing into the current and letting it take me—fishing pole in hand—wherever it might. I remembered fires on the banks at night. The sound of a hoot owl. And the smell of late-summer blackberries. All things that now didn't seem possible. Unless . . .

One shot.

I looked at the flames and fingered the pistol, a P38 I'd picked up from a German we'd taken prisoner in Holland. One shot and I'd be back to all that. Not a shot in the head, though a few soldiers were known to do that, too. But in the foot. Hell, there's no sugarcoating it: This was a coward's way out. It wasn't common, but it happened in war: One squeeze of the trigger and you'd be unable to fight. You'd be a liability to your company, so they'd have no choice but to ship you back to the safety of England, maybe even the States. Accidents happen.

But would the guys really buy that your gun had *accidentally* gone off? Don Hoobler's had just yesterday, but he bled to death on the way to an aid station. I'd make sure I missed a main artery. Regardless, the price for my ticket home would be my integrity. All these guys forever wondering, *Did Malark do it on purpose?* But, then, integrity is an easy thing to lose in times of war, accidentally or on purpose. And when you watch others lose theirs, it becomes easier to let go of your own. Hell, back near Utah Beach, you'd see the bodies of soldiers stacked up like so much cordwood. Where's the integrity in that? Or hear those stories about 1st Lt. Ronald Speirs gunning down a bunch of German prisoners, even one of his own men, some say. Where's the integrity in that? Or even before the war, at Fort Benning, watch the drumming-out ceremonies. The guys who couldn't cut it—the guys who weren't going to make paratroopers—would be marched up in front of everybody with a tommy gun at their backs and an officer would strip them of basically everything they had, including their pride. Where was the integrity in that?

In war, you quickly realize that you're playing a game of odds. The longer you fight, the better chance you have of something bad happening to you. You die. You get wounded. You get sick. You get captured. Or you quit.

Like my father. He quit. Not in war. But in life. Went bankrupt during the Depression—he was an insurance man—and just quit. Quit trying. Quit caring. Quit noticing anything and anybody around him. When times got tough, when he lost his business, my dad was like some twenty-foot runabout trying to get over the bar at the mouth of the Columbia: crushed to splinters.

My father missed World War I because he had been 90 percent blind in one eye; he was 4F so he worked in a spruce mill making airplane parts. But World War I took the lives of two of my uncles, his brothers. Though I never knew them, they were my heroes. I felt a bond with them both. So much of a bond, in fact, that when learning that Easy Company would be shipping out, ultimately to fight the Germans, I felt the need to somehow avenge their deaths. To bring back something—some symbol—that would tell my family, *I did it. I evened the slate.* Some sort of souvenir. Like the pistol whose hammer, in the chill of the Ardennes Forest, I now cocked.

Truth is, I'd gotten to this point for reasons beyond Joe Toye and Bill Guarnere getting their legs blown off. Beyond missing the Nehalem River, I also missed Bernice Franetovich, a girl I'd known from Astoria who was now living in New York, where she was a singer. I'd started to wonder if it was only a matter of time before everyone in Easy Company was going to wind up like those frozen Germans you'd have to all but step over when heading to an outpost. We were like the shipwrecked sailors on a raft, waiting for the sharks.

I felt hopeless. Numb. Not from the cold, as I'd been since we'd arrived in this god-awful forest December 19, but from something that chills you far deeper inside you: death. We'd lost more than a dozen guys in the last few weeks, some of whom were my friends. You see a dead enemy soldier and you say, *At least it wasn't one of ours.* You see a dead American soldier —one of your own—and you say, *At least it wasn't me.* You lose a friend and you say, *To hell with this. Get me out of here.* At the same time, though this might sound strange, you almost envy the peace they now have. No more being cold. No more war. No more pain. All that bad stuff gets left to those of us who remain.

Things started swirling in my mind, like a cottonwood bud caught in an eddy on the Nehalem. I didn't say anything because there are certain things soldiers don't talk about. Like a lot of other jabs of pain—say, the time after we'd gotten back from Normandy when our laundry woman kept handing me clothes for dead guys who weren't going to be needing them—I stuffed it deep inside, thinking it would somehow just go away. It didn't. It just builds up, like carrying one more brick on your back, and one more, and more, and more. And finally you say, *Enough. I can't walk another step.*

So I found myself standing in front of that fire, which was

growing weaker and weaker as the late afternoon grew darker and darker. Somewhere out there, the enemy still lurked, waiting for morning—and me. And somewhere inside me, another enemy lurked as well, waiting for my decision. Soldiers around me smoked cigarettes and made small talk, but I didn't hear a word of it. Instead, I stared at the embers, mesmerized. Slowly, my right forefinger curled around the pistol's icy trigger.

2

BOMBA THE JUNGLE BOY

Astoria, Oregon
July 1921 to September 1939

Maybe it was what they call destiny, a sign of what would become of me in the future. Then again, maybe it was just me being little Donnie Malarkey and doing a damn-fool thing because I always had a little of the devil in me. All I know is that when I was about twelve years old, at a time when nobody in Astoria, Oregon, or hardly anywhere else in the world had heard of a man jumping out of an airplane while wearing something called a parachute, I jumped off the roof of our house on Kensington Avenue, clutching only a beach umbrella.

How I didn't bust myself all to hell is beyond me. I just remember trying to avoid hitting the concrete walkway and somehow surviving the jump with only minor injuries that I didn't dare confess to my mother, Helen. And, afterward, believing more fervently in the law of gravity than in the ability of a five-foot-wide umbrella to float an eighty-pound kid fifteen feet to the ground.

Besides being one of the more daring kids in Astoria, I was the best marble player. As kids, we'd gather in vacant lots and shoot marbles, and I'd win over and over. On Saturday mornings, I'd stand on our front porch, and as kids came by, I'd toss back all the marbles I'd won from them during the week. I still remember some mother yelling at me, "You, Malarkey boy, come *here*!" Some of our games were for money, and I guess I'd won a little lunch money from her kid.

But marbles, if good business, weren't as exciting as more physical pursuits. My pals and I played war behind the house in a forest that seemed to stretch on forever. And I dreamed of someday playing football and basketball for Astoria High, the vaunted Fishermen, whose rival down the coast was the Seaside Sandfleas. Basketball, in particular, was big in Astoria; seems like every telephone pole had a rim nailed to it, though you had to be careful because much of the town was notched into a hill overlooking the Columbia River and a runaway ball could wind up at the fish canneries fourteen blocks away.

Astoria won three state basketball championships in the midthirties. A couple of Astoria players on those teams, Bobby Anet and Wally Johanson, would go on to the University of Oregon and, in 1939, help the school win the first NCAA championship ever held. As a kid, I watched practically every game they played at Astoria High and wanted badly to play for the Fishermen someday.

Meanwhile, I not only thirsted for adventure, but found it. Winters in Astoria usually meant rain followed by more rain; seventy-inch years weren't uncommon. Growing up, I had no less than eleven ear infections that required lancing because of our dank winters. Summers were far better, particularly a bit inland, where our family's tented cabin was on the Nehalem River, about thirty-five miles from town.

I would swim for what seemed like miles on a summer day up and down that river, my only audience the alder and fir and hemlock that lined the snaking waters. I imagined myself as an Indian living off the land. I'd row my boat upriver half a mile, make camp, build a fire, and stay the night. Trap chipmunks. Hunt with my yew-wood bow. Climb a ridge to Lost Lake. I was a curly-blond-haired Huck Finn, an independent cuss living the life of Riley.

Beyond the books I had to read at St. Mary's Star of the Sea School—and a few, about poetry, which I actually *liked*—there was one set that I buried my head in night after night: the *Bomba the Jungle Boy* series by Roy Rockwood. The books started coming out in the midtwenties just as I was learning to read. They included titles like *Bomba the Jungle Boy in the Swamp of Death* and *Bomba the Jungle Boy in a Strange Land.*

I loved those books. I *lived* those books. I was the Bomba of Astoria, Oregon—at least in my mind. At the corner of Fifteenth and Madison, a massive growth of alder saplings ran kitty-corner to Fourteenth and Lexington. I would climb up those slim alder trees and start swinging on a branch until it propelled me forward a bit. You'd let go of that branch and grab hold of the trunk of another tree, and before you knew it, you'd gone an entire block without touching the ground. Amazing!

Astoria is known as the place where the explorers Lewis and Clark ended their journey west, then turned around. As a little boy, I'd read their journals—in Astoria, kids were spoon-fed Lewis and Clark as if it were our morning Malt-O-Meal—and how some of the men in the Corps of Discovery were going mad, mainly because of the never-ending rain and eight guys crammed into twenty-by-twenty log-built rooms at Fort Clatsop, just across Young's Bay from where I lived.

It's the oldest American settlement west of the Rockies, founded in 1847, a few decades after John Jacob Astor, a rich New Yorker, first established it as a fur-trading outpost. By the time I was born, fur was no longer the draw. Instead, it was fish, lumber, and farming. The town lay mainly on a hillside in Oregon's far northwest corner, surrounded by water everywhere: the mighty Columbia River, separating Oregon from Washington; the Pacific Ocean to the west; and Young's Bay.

It was a raw, rugged world that never let you forget life was tough, dangerous, and sometimes deadly. Logging, fishing, and shipping freight across an ocean weren't for the lighthearted. You'd show up for school one day and the kid who sat next to you wouldn't be there; he'd be at the funeral for his dad the logger, who'd been crushed by a widow maker. The Columbia's bar at Astoria, with swells to forty feet, was known as the Graveyard of the Pacific. And if we needed any reminding of such dangers, we could always see the skeletal remains of the *Peter Iredale*, a four-masted British sailing vessel that had gone aground in 1906 on the Clatsop Spit.

There were pockets of sophistication in Astoria, a lot of old-money families who lived in the ornate Victorian houses perched on Coxcomb Hill. But, for the most part, Astoria in the twenties and thirties was the smell of fish canneries and salt air and lumber mills and dairy farms. Of blackberries, cedar trees, and, of course, the crap that was dumped straight into the Columbia River from all our homes. It was the sound of ship whistles, seagulls, log trucks rolling down Commercial Street, and rain tapping on our windows, day after day after day after winter day.

Astoria was warehouses jutting out over the river on pilings, brawls outside the bars and brothels of Astor Street, the Salmon Derby each August, playing baseball in the field notched into the hill behind Star of the Sea School, and a mix of people as different as the ingredients in a bowl of fisherman's stew. The Finns lived in the west part of town, nearest the Pacific Ocean, which pounded ashore about ten miles away. The Danes, Swedes, and Norwegians lived in east Astoria, up into the hills. The Irish, including the Malarkeys, lived in the center.

Our house was a bungalow near the top of the hill, 595 Kensington Avenue, that had a white chimney, smack in front, not off to the side like most houses. That chimney looked almost like a lighthouse. We had a great view of the barges and tugs—white-water cowboys, we called 'em— pulling and pushing rafts of logs; ferries going to and from Megler, Washington, five miles across the river; and ships heading to and from Portland, about sixty miles upriver. To the east of us, on the corner of Kensington and Fourteenth, lived a rugged man named Michael Nolan, a bar pilot, one of the guys who guided ships over the feared Columbia River bar. From his porch, he would tell us all sorts of stories. Of shipwrecks. Of miraculous recoveries. Of rogue waves three stories high.

Though not rich by any means, we were better off than a lot of folks during the Depression. My father, Leo, owned an insurance business in an office above the Liberty Theater on Commercial Avenue. I still remember his ads: "Tick

Malarkey: That Man Insures Anything," a slogan that the *Evening Astorian-Budget* would say "was for a long time as familiar to local citizens as the Columbia River or Coxcomb Hill." He picked up the nickname at the University of Oregon, where he played football. As part of his athletic scholarship, it was his job to wind the clock at Villard Hall. Thus, "Tick." He made enough money to send us to Star of the Sea and my brother John to prep school in Portland. Also enough so he could play golf, and my mom, bridge, at the country club.

I was born July 31, 1921, one of four children. John, about two years older than me, taught me to fish on the Nehalem, near our family cabin, when I was six. Bob was five years younger. Marilyn—I called her Molly, and it stuck—was fifteen years younger.

My father wasn't around much. When we were at the cabin, he would work in town and come out on Wednesday nights. Then he'd go back to work two days and return to the cabin for the weekends. So, most of the time, it was my mom and my brothers and me.

Besides my brother John, Louie Jacobson taught me outdoor stuff, too, like how to shoot a bow and arrow and trap a chipmunk. He was half-Indian. The way I spent so much time in the woods, some people joked that I was full-blooded. I remember shooting what I thought was my first quail. When I ran to where it had nose-dived into some tall grass, I realized it wasn't a quail after all, but a robin. I felt like two cents.

Sometimes I was made to feel bad even when I hadn't done anything wrong. Like when I got nabbed by a Catholic nun at school for carrying around a chipmunk in my shirt pocket. I don't know why she was mad; I hadn't killed the little critter. Still, an angry nun was nothing compared to the terror I felt one day in the summer of 1933, when I was twelve.

My father had gotten me a job on a dairy farm outside town, on land where our cabin was, working with Jack Bay's nephew, Einar Glaser. Einar, in his midtwenties, was the strongest man I knew; he made Charles Atlas look like a weakling. I started every day at 5:30 A.M., milking cows, then cleaning the barns, and, finally, delivering milk in Einar's old Chevy pickup. I enjoyed the job; it made me feel important. Out on the Sunset Highway we'd deliver milk to logging camps and a construction company. The logging companies would send riders on horseback to pick up their orders. One day, while on a delivery, I was in a camp mess hall, eating a cookie and drinking a glass of milk—a cook named Oney Kelly always pampered me—when an out-of-breath farmer burst through the door.

"Everybody out!" he shouted. "Forest fire's headin' this way! Headin' for Ben Gronnell's place."

We fled west, down Sunset Highway and back to the dairy farm. I spent the entire day with a bucket in my hands, dipping water from Lost Lake Creek and dispersing it to farmers as they yelled for it, trying to save the farm. And we did. My hands were bleeding from the handles on the pails; I'm surprised any water was left in that stream, given how fast we were working, but it made me feel sort of heroic, like a real man instead of a little kid. I'd been up since sunup. It was now about 10:00 P.M. Finally, my boss, Mr. Glaser, drove me back to our family cabin. My folks were worried sick, which made me feel a little guilty and a little good at the same time, if you know what I mean.

I got a sandwich and some water to drink, then went to bed; my brother Bob and I had a double bunk. An hour later, I heard people stirring.

"Bob, Donnie, get up!" my father shouted. "Fire's comin'."

The winds had shifted. Our cabin was smack in the middle of an old-growth Douglas fir forest. Limbs were torching into fireballs and falling far too close for comfort. You could hear the crackle, nearly feel the heat. We threw everything we could into the car and a little trailer—I took the stuff I valued most, my camping gear—then all five of us headed out to a hundred-acre hayfield that had been harvested. Safe from the fire. I remember being under this old wooden wagon. I lay there all night long in a sleeping bag, watching this wall of flames gradually gobble up trees and head for our cabin. About 3:00 A.M., a fireball exploded on Red Bluff, across the Nehalem. By morning, we all knew what we later confirmed: Our cabin was gone, swallowed by what would become known as the Tillamook Burn, one of the largest forest fires ever to burn in the United States. In one night, that wall of flame traveled thirty-five miles and took away the one thing that meant more to me than just about anything else. Just like that, our cabin: gone.

I would lose other things in my life in the same sort of way: here one moment, gone the next. I would lose other things more gradually. Like my father.

We were proud to be Irish. Proud to be Malarkeys. And proud to be Americans. When needed, Malarkeys served their country. I never knew my uncles, but I grew up with the stories about them and felt as if I knew them. Stories about how Gerald had died in France; he was barely nineteen.

Stories about how Bob was gassed in the Argonne Forest. He survived and came back from the war, coached football for a year at Stanford, and spent the rest of his life being shipped from one veterans' hospital to another. His lungs were like burnt toast. He died at thirty-one.

My uncles were legends in Astoria and revered in our home. In my eyes, they were the equal of Babe Ruth, Lou Gehrig, Notre Dame football, and the marvelous basketball teams at Astoria High. The scrapbooks with stories about Gerald and Bob were permanent fixtures in our living room. I looked at them often, showed them to my pals. On July 10, 1918, my grandfather Daniel Malarkey wrote to his son Gerald in France:

I do not know when you will be at the Front. However, I wish to state that, were I your age, I WOULD BE THERE. I have every confidence that you will acquit yourself like a true American and that fortified by your Catholic Faith you will be prepared for anything that may befall. Son, you are as much a crusader as any knight of old who wore the cross and went to battle with the slogan "God wills it." Therefore, notwithstanding the tender heart of your dear Mother, don't forget that we both want you to do your full duty and know that you will.

Gerald died almost a month later to the day, in Château-Thierry in eastern France, on August 11, 1918. He'd been hit by shrapnel from a German shell. He was barely nineteen, the first soldier from Clatsop County to die in World War I. At the request of the mayor, businesses closed for one hour for his memorial service at Ocean View Cemetery in Warrenton. *The Oregonian* newspaper in Portland, where

Gerald had briefly attended prep school, wrote he was "a mild tempered, quiet, lovable young fellow . . . talented and painstaking in his studies, strenuous and enthusiastic on the athletic field." An army honor guard, the Astoria paper reported, "fired a parting salute to the youngster who proved his mettle when his country called and who, in asking permission of his parents to enlist, said simply, 'Somebody must go.'"

My other uncle's death from World War I was painstakingly slow. Bob was playing football at the University of Oregon when, as a sophomore, he enlisted. After struggling to survive for years after being gassed in France, he came to be known as Fighting Bob. One Portland newspaper columnist said when told he was going to die, Bob said, "Tell me another funny story. I'm just starting to fight." In 1926, my grandfather Dan Malarkey was in Denver at the bedside of his dying son. He sent this Western Union telegram to my father:

> Chaplain Sliney and I were called to Robert's bedside at two this morning. He is growing gradually weaker. His mental attitude is inspiring and it is his request that I send this message (stop) He is fully resigned to the will of God (stop) If he is to pass at this time he begs of you all, especially Mother, Edith [his wife] and his sisters not to grieve unduly for he will be released from suffering and at peace (stop) He sends his dear wife undying love and blesses Mother for all she has been to him (stop)

His death made big news in both Portland and Astoria. He was buried next to his brother, Gerald, at Ocean View.

The *Evening Astorian-Budget* wrote an editorial called "Two Graves":

Today, the tired, battle-scarred, pain-racked body of Robert Malarkey is laid to rest amid the peaceful dunes of Ocean View. The new made grave close beside an older one beneath whose mound there lies in sleep eternal his younger brother, Gerald, who died on the field of Château Thierry.

In those graves there lie the broken bodies of two young heroes and there, too, the broken hopes of a father and mother. There is grief and sorrow there, but there is pride and joy, too, and there is victory and triumph and glory. But there must be something more than this if "the dead shall know that they have not fall'n in vain" and if the mourning parents shall know that the big price they have been called to pay is not wasted. Those graves and others like them must remind us that peace is the fruit of war and that the victory such graves have bought is a vast defeat unless it shall become an enduring victory for the cause of peace.

Because I wasn't even alive when Gerald died and only five when Bob died, I never mourned their deaths. But in hearing and reading about them, I took a pride in my uncles that I didn't take even in my own father. In part, that's probably why I felt so close to their mother, Ida, my grandmother Malarkey. The reasons for my feeling so distant from my father were far more complex.

My father, Leo, met my mother, Helen Trask, in Portland when he was a college sports reporter for *The Oregonian* newspaper. They were married in 1918. She was a gracious lady who worked hard, loved her family, and remained loyal to the man she married, which couldn't have been easy.

My father was a well-liked guy with a life-of-the-party personality; at the University of Oregon, he starred as a halfback on the football team, though an eye injury forced him to miss his senior year. So he became an assistant coach; in fact, he coached his brother Bob, a starting halfback, in 1916, the season the University of Oregon beat the University of Pennsylvania in the Rose Bowl.

The best thing about my father was hearing him tell stories of his being a football hero. He drank a lot; he was, after all, Irish. But, early on, I don't recall its being a big problem, other than the time he came home loaded and made some slanderous remarks in front of my mom's sister, or the time he walked into the Liberty Grill on Commercial Street, where I was busing dishes as a high school senior. He looked at me and said, loud enough for everyone to hear, "There's my no-good son." You don't forget something like that. Ever.

Mom was a loving woman and the family disciplinarian. She gave us our chores. She took us to church every Sunday at St. Mary's Parish, where I served as an altar boy. She also took us berry picking along the Nehalem. I loved to pick blackberries and blueberries. It was much more fun than being an altar boy and, for a kid who felt most alive when he was outdoors, was maybe the place I felt closer to God, too. Those were the happiest times: me and my mom and sister and brothers out picking berries. Pick three. Eat one, throw one at a brother or sister, and save one for jam. Your hands and face would be the color of deep bruises, and it smelled good and life was safe and easy.

But the Depression changed everything. With money

short, in the summer when I was fifteen I started working at a seining ground located on a tidal island fifteen miles up the Columbia called Jim Crow Sands, on the Oregon side of the river. The salmon were so thick people joked you could walk from Oregon to Washington on their backs. Our job was to corral them in nets and get them in boats. Until I ran up and down a mountain in Georgia called Currahee, it was the hardest work I'd ever done. I was a boy among men.

The seines were laid out by two tugs. One pulled the head of the net, the other the tail. When full, the nets were towed to the sandbar, where the tail of the net was passed to a team of horses that pulled the half-moon configuration in until the net was compact enough so our crews could get at the fish. Some of the salmon were nearly the size of ironing boards—and up to fifty pounds. We'd transfer the fish into wooden boats called "slimes" that would transport the catch to the canneries. We lived in logging camp–style rooms and were paid $3 a day, plus a fifty-cents-a-day bonus if we lasted the whole season. I did. For three summers.

In 1938, my father's insurance business, like the occasional dead chinook or sockeye we'd find in our nets, went belly-up. Bankrupt. He was a good salesman but a terrible bill-collector. He trusted people too much. Didn't want to go after money that was owed him. And I admired him for that. Hell, you can't blame someone for being blown over in a storm. But you can blame them for not even trying to get back up.

Months later, we lost the house. The folks told us they were moving out to a replacement cabin in the Cow Creek Valley, not far from our old one that had burned down. John, my older brother, was already living in southern California with relatives, but Bob, then thirteen, and Molly, three, were going with Mom and Dad. I would live with Grandmother Malarkey in Warrenton, across Young's Bay.

There went our family. There went my friends in Astoria. There went my dreams of playing basketball at Astoria High; I'd made Catholic All-State in basketball for two years at Star of the Sea, but though I'd transferred to Astoria for my senior year, it was impossible to live in Warrenton and find rides home from practice each night; instead, I played intramurals.

It's not that I didn't like living with Grandma Malarkey. She was a wonderful human being. She was that woman who'd be visiting all the down-and-out folks who needed visiting. She had a certain holiness to her, almost as if she were a saint. She lived on Main Street in a yellow, two-story bungalow shaded by Douglas firs and fronted by a white picket fence, with a huge garden out back. But she was recently widowed. She'd already raised her children, two of whom had been taken by World War I, and now she was being asked to do it again—at age sixty-four.

Meanwhile, my father retreated deeper and deeper into the dark, like a hermit crab wedged deep in the crevice of a couple of rocks, watching but seldom coming out. Years later, after he died, *The Oregonian* newspaper would say he "retired because of ill health in 1940." But I don't remember him being sick. I just remember him going numb as if he didn't want anything to do with any of us, partly because of the bankruptcy and partly because of the bottle he relied on to make him forget the bankruptcy. He was not exactly the guy who the *Evening Astorian-Budget* had once reported had endeared himself to the University of Oregon football coach because of his *fight*. "Malarkey literally works himself to death on the field," a reporter had written. "When it is just about dark, and that is the time that [Coach Hugo] Bezdek says nowadays, 'take a lap around the track easy and then go in on the jump,' 'Tick' has just as much pep as ever."

He and my mother weren't separated by law, but by every other measure. Mom would stay in the cabin and he'd spend time in Warrenton or Astoria, doing who-knows-what. So with John gone, I became the one who had to help keep the family together, financially and otherwise. That's not why I was disappointed in my father. I could deal with having to take on more responsibility. What I couldn't deal with was my father giving up on himself. On life. On us.

I don't remember thinking, *I'll never be like my old man.* Looking back on it, I believe somewhere down deep I vowed I would never do what he did. No matter how bad it got, I would never quit. On myself. Or on those around me.

As a high school student, I would never have been confused with my grandmother the saint. Oh, I wasn't a big-time hell-raiser, but if some garbage cans were getting kicked around on Halloween, you could bet my buddies and I were somehow involved. We rolled a few tires down from Fourteenth and Jerome, which was a little like rolling tires off an Olympic ski jump. When Leland Wesley, at Star of the Sea School, made a rank remark about my girlfriend, Bernice Franetovich, I slammed him against the wall and threatened to kick the hell out of him. Bernice and I had pretty much fallen for each other ever since freshman initiation when we were blindfolded and I took her hand to help her up the stairs.

I suppose I had a touch of rebel spirit in me, probably more so after our family broke up and I moved to Warrenton. I began smoking, not that other guys didn't. Music was a

more serious addiction. The Big Bands. Glenn Miller. Tommy
Dorsey. We'd gather at the house of someone who was a good
piano player, like Bernice. Or go somewhere to listen to records. Or belt out a few songs around a beach fire some Saturday night, if the wind wasn't blowing us from here to hell's
half acre as it often was.

Not to brag, but I was a pretty decent singer. Before the big
split, my mother would have me sing to her. In 1939, when
Dorsey came out with that "Hawaiian War Chant" song, I
could nail it, tricky though it was. In the midst of the Depression, music was a release. Music was like salvation. Music
made you forget that life was no longer as simple as rowing
up the Nehalem to find a good place to build a fire and
camp for the evening.

At Star of the Sea, a Catholic school with thirty pupils, I
was a decent student. The nuns made sure of that. Math was
not their strong suit, but they pounded the other subjects
into you, especially English. They made you break down sen-
tences and examine every part as if you were some sort of
word detective. They had us sing until we all thought we belonged onstage, and memorize poetry, which I actually
learned to enjoy.

As a senior, I was allowed to transfer to Astoria High,
though an injury wiped out football for me and I couldn't
play basketball because of the difficulty of getting a ride for
the ten miles to and from Warrenton. Once, a teacher asked
our class if we'd read the editorial in the previous day's
Evening Astoria-Budget about the possibilities of Adolf Hitler
invading the Low Countries—Belgium, Luxembourg, and
the Netherlands. I was the only one who had.

Bernice's father, Louie—he'd come from Croatia—ran the
Liberty Grill on Commercial Street and I got a job there as a

busboy. Her dad seemed to think I was OK and I thought he was, too. In 1922, the Astoria Fire had leveled most of downtown, but in a time when a lot of people gave up, he rebuilt. I always admired that, along with the Grill's hamburger steak and mashed potatoes. The Grill also made wonderful clam chowder, heavy on the clams. Once, when President Franklin Roosevelt went salmon fishing on the Columbia, his aides would motor ashore and bring him back Liberty Grill chowder, on his request. Bernice was proud of her dad for that, and who could blame her?

One day at the Liberty Grill, this bar pilot looked up from his newspaper and asked me what I thought Germany was going to do with France. He was surprised that I actually had an answer.

"Germany," I said, "is like the Notre Dame of Europe. Powerful. France and all of Europe is in big trouble."

The next day, Louie, the owner, told me a guy had overheard me talking about Germany at the counter yesterday. He was with the FBI, and sure enough this guy wanted to know how I knew so much about the war in Europe, which seemed odd because I'd just been reading the papers. It was a time of great suspicion, those late thirties. The world seemed on the brink of something bad, but we just weren't sure what that something was.

I graduated from Astoria High in the spring of 1939, and with my father and mother not working, I had no money to attend the University of Oregon, my school of choice. So I decided I'd put myself through school on my own. I got a job loading ships and blending flour at the Pillsbury Flour Mill in Astoria, at the time one of the country's largest-volume export mills to the Far East. I stowed some money away for college and bought a '36 Chevrolet.

I left grandma's house and lived in an apartment that Bernice's father owned on Franklin Avenue. Bernice was still my girl; when she was selected as a princess in the Queen's Court of the Astoria Regatta, she naturally chose me as her escort. I worked at the mill during the day and bused dishes at the Liberty Grill at night. One foggy September evening—on the northern-Oregon coast, no month is safe from the stuff—I was cleaning up a table when I saw a copy of *The Evening Astoria-Budget*, its front page ringed with the circles of a few coffee cups and its main headline tinged with dread:

FIGHTING UNDERWAY

I had the same feeling I had had when the farmer had burst into the doors of that camp mess hall to tell us a forest fire was headed our way.

3

"MOM, DON'T WORRY, I'LL BE BACK"

Eugene and Astoria, Oregon
September 1939 to September 1942

I entered the University of Oregon in the fall of 1941, having worked two years and sold my car to afford it. I'd almost been predestined to go to UO, given the pipeline between Eugene and my older Astoria friends, and my dad and uncle Bob having gone there. The college was about 150 miles southeast of Astoria, at the lower end of the Willamette Valley.

Eugene was lush, rainy, but not nearly as wet as what I'd been used to, and sprinkled liberally with Douglas fir trees and coeds with beautiful legs. Elsewhere in the world, Germany, after the Czechoslovakia takeover and the conquest of Poland, was taking over countries with a sort of devil-may-care arrogance: Denmark, Norway, France, Belgium, Luxembourg, the Netherlands, and others—and bombing the hell out of Great Britain. America instituted a peacetime draft because President Franklin Roosevelt supported Great Britain, which had declared war on Germany after its invasion of Poland. America was sending the British money, weapons, and machinery. The common thinking was that America's involvement in this war wasn't a matter of *if*, but *when*. Meanwhile, I tried to ignore the possibilities.

In some ways, college was like a grown-up version of life on the Nehalem. An escape of sorts. I joined the Sigma Nu fraternity on Eleventh Street, where my father and uncle Bob had been members back in the teens. I still worked— this time, washing dishes at the fraternity and at a sorority, which, for obvious reasons, was more fun than working at my own house. Both jobs were far easier than tossing around thirty-pound salmon or loading cargo ships. I partied, sang with the fraternity choir, and watched football games at Hayward Field and basketball games at McArthur Court. I even went to classes regularly, deciding to get a degree in business administration.

Bernice, who'd gone a year to Marylhurst College in Portland, transferred to Oregon when I began there. We dated for a while, but she hadn't pledged a sorority and I took so much ribbing from my fraternity brothers that I broke up with her. That was a stupid reason to part, but when you're young, sometimes you do stupid things.

What I remember most about that first year, other than a mandatory Reserve Officers' Training Corps (ROTC) class all male students were required to take because of the war in Europe, were a couple of poems I memorized. On my entrance exam for the University of Oregon, I remember being told I was among the few newcomers who wouldn't need to take bonehead English because Star of the Sea had prepared me so well. One poem I learned at Oregon was Milton's "On His Blindness." Another was "Gunga Din," by Rudyard Kipling, about this water boy during war who earns the praise of his military master. It reminded me of a certain twelve-year-old boy carrying buckets of water out of Lost Lake Creek to help save a man's farm. I didn't think it was all that emotional a poem, but when I recited it in a freshman English class, two students in the front row were in tears.

The other poem I loved, by William Ernest Henley, was called "Invictus":

> Out of the night that covers me,
> Black as the Pit from pole to pole,
> I thank whatever gods may be
> For my unconquerable soul.
>
> In the fell clutch of circumstance
> I have not winced nor cried aloud.
> Under the bludgeonings of chance
> My head is bloody, but unbowed.
>
> Beyond this place of wrath and tears
> Looms but the Horror of the shade,
> And yet the menace of the years
> Finds, and shall find, me unafraid.
>
> It matters not how strait the gate,
> How charged with punishments the scroll,
> I am the master of my fate:
> I am the captain of my soul.

It's strange how when you're young and learning stuff, you never stop to think that someday you might use whatever it is you're learning. But even though, in the thirties, I thought "Invictus" was little more than an inspiring poem about not giving up, I would—in war—find a strength in those words that sometimes got me through another day.

"You don't seem like the poetry type," one of my fraternity brothers once told me.

"I know, you think of me more like the Frank Sinatra type," I said, laughing.

One Sunday morning in early December, I was washing pots and pans left over from a Saturday-night dinner at the house when a fraternity brother rushed in.

"The Japs have bombed Pearl Harbor!" he said.

"Where the hell is Pearl Harbor?" I asked, a naive question for a guy who'd been acing geography all through school.

The big question in the fraternity that week was what branch of the service we were each headed for. Fall term wound to a close. I took my finals, though I missed an ROTC test because I was in the student infirmary with yet another ear infection. Then I packed for my trip home, knowing, down the road, I'd be off to war in some way, shape, or form. I was a Malarkey. That's just what we did. Never thought twice about finding some way out, even though I would soon be offered one.

Everywhere you went, talk was of the war. I had a good friend from Astoria who was also going to school at the University of Oregon, a Japanese kid named Tom Hayashi. He was an excellent swimmer and basketball player. His folks ran some kind of store. Shortly after the bombing, I saw him leaning against the wall of the library, near a bunch of phones. He was crying.

"What's the matter, Tommy?" I asked.

He paused a moment and shook his head a bit. "Just talked to my folks back in Astoria. People are throwing rocks through the windows at their store." The idea sickened me. I never saw him again; like most Japanese during those times, he was probably soon shipped off to one of those internment camps.

On December 15, I hitchhiked north to Portland and was in the bus depot when I noticed a Marine Corps recruiting sign across the street. What the heck; I had a little time to kill, so I sauntered over and took a physical exam. The doctor said I was 100 percent fit—except for one thing. After checking my mouth, he said my teeth weren't up to snuff. No explanation. (Many years later, I learned the marines had a regulation about having so many of your back molars—something to do with a medical device they would put in your mouth to knock you out for surgery—and I was a few short of regulation.)

I hopped on a bus headed for Astoria and was reading the November 1941 edition of *Reader's Digest*. Among the articles was one about something called paratroopers, soldiers the United States was training in Georgia to jump out of airplanes, land, and fight. Said the article:

> Soldiers chosen must be unmarried, under 30, physically tops and emotionally well balanced. When one of these picked men reaches Fort Benning he starts through the toughest school ever devised for American soldiers. For six weeks he is hardened into a physical

superman, driven through exercises which make football practice look soft. . . . They are probably the hardest, toughest and best-dressed soldiers in the Army. . . .
When he gets his jump training he gets silver wings to
wear on his blouse and he is cocky.

Thank God I'd flunked the Marine Corps physical. I
knew, at that moment, that being a paratrooper was for me.
I wanted to be one of the hardest, toughest, and best-
dressed soldiers in the army. I wanted to be "hardened into
a physical superman." Wear those wings. Hell, I wanted to
jump out of an airplane with a parachute on my back and be
"cocky." It seemed challenging, yet simple: go on a mission
for few days, fight like hell, get picked up, and return to
your post.

I arrived home for the holidays to the Cow Creek cabin.
With nothing but the Pacific Ocean between Oregon and
Japan, a touch of tenseness was in the air that hadn't been
there before. The Japanese had attacked Hawaii; what
would prevent them from bombing the mainland United
States? And Astoria was a major shipping port at the mouth
of the largest West Coast river to empty into the Pacific. The
army had already commandeered one of Astoria's two ferries to use as a mine layer at the mouth of the Columbia.

I mentioned my plan to become a paratrooper to my
mother. She broke down on the spot. Three weeks of being
at war had a lot of folks jittery about their sons. Hearing that
I wasn't interested in a desk job but wanted to jump out of
airplanes caught her off guard.

My grandmother took it even harder. She was a Gold Star
Mother who had already lost two sons, my uncles, to war.
Now the worries of war she'd experienced two decades ago

were suddenly back, thanks to me. For the rest of my time at home, the proverbial elephant was in the room. I didn't want to talk about it. Neither did my mom or grandmother. So we didn't. I can't remember seeing my father; as I said, he was usually just somewhere else.

When I returned to Eugene for winter term, I got a kick below the belt: My ROTC instructor, Colonel Swanson, had given me an F. Flunked me for missing that fall-term final.

"You need to repeat the course, young man," he said.

Repeat? "But I missed the test because I was in bed in the infirmary, sir," I said. "I *couldn't* be there."

"That's not good enough."

"I'm sorry, but I had A's all fall. Can't I just take the test? I can prove that—"

"You'll need to repeat the course, Mr. Malarkey," he said with a this-discussion-is-over tone to his voice.

"But—"

"Look, young man, we're at war and I'm tired of fooling with college students who don't seem to appreciate that *fact*."

Something welled up deep within. I was a Malarkey. I was from Astoria, home of tough, proud, independent cusses who believed, at their core, in a square deal—and this didn't seem too square. I turned my back, marched to the Sigma Nu house, got my olive drab army uniform, and returned to his office.

His receptionist tried to stop me. I blew right past her, dropped that uniform on his desk, and walked away. Swanson didn't say a word. Neither did I. Heading down Thirteenth Street back to the house, I suddenly realized what I'd done, even if I tried to tell myself that it was the right thing. Even if my pride was clouding what I didn't want to face.

I'd done exactly what I said I wouldn't do.

I'd quit.

Winter and spring terms had a heaviness to them, like the battleship-gray clouds that seemed to roll across the Coast Range, and into Eugene, about November and overstay their welcome until May. It wasn't so much because of the past—my dropping out of ROTC—but because of the future. The world was at war, and now America was in the thick of it. An Allied invasion of France was a distinct possibility.

In April, home for a break, I again mentioned the idea of my becoming a paratrooper. And again my mother turned icy. "You know what happened to your uncles," she said. Yeah, I knew, and, in some ways, I was thinking, *That's exactly why I need to join. The Malarkeys have some unfinished business with the Germans.* Of course, I didn't say that to her.

"Mom," I said. "Don't worry, I'll be back."

Then I wavered a bit on my paratrooper decision. Maybe to appease her and Grandmother Malarkey—maybe to appease myself since I'd been smitten with being a pilot since another of my uncles, Cecil Eckert, had taken me flying as a kid in Portland—I later took an exam for pilot training with the Army Air Corps at the University of Oregon. But the math was beyond me; nothing at Star of the Sea had prepared me for this. I walked out in midtest.

I registered for the draft, finished my freshman year at Oregon—my transcript showed three straight flunks for ROTC—and moved to Portland to work in a machinery shop, Monarch Forge and Machine Works. The plant did extensive work for Liberty ships, the vessels that would ferry our troops to battle. As a machinist, I helped make propeller shafts. A few years before, amid the thousands of men and women working in similar plants in Portland, one young man about my age worked across the street at Schmitz Steel Company. I never met him, but I would meet him in a couple of years, in Normandy, on what would come to be known as D-day. I would be wearing the uniform of an American paratrooper. He would be wearing the uniform of the enemy.

In July, as I turned twenty-one, my draft notice arrived, but there were still some outs. My boss at Monarch offered me a deferment. I could, he told me, fulfill my military obligation by continuing to work in the plant. I thanked him, but refused. Weeks later, papers came instructing me to report to Fort Lewis, a few hours north, near Tacoma. I quit my job and went home to spend a few days with my mother and grandmother. Bernice was off at some special music school.

While there, I ran into an old buddy who was home on leave from Fort Lewis. He told me the first thing they asked for was volunteers to be in the paratroopers.

"Whatever you do, don't say yes, Malarkey," he said. "It's a death sentence. You're jumpin' out of a friggin' airplane going a couple hundred miles an hour—and right into enemy territory. The odds stink."

But I'd made up my mind: That's what I was going to do. He shook his head sideways. "You're nuts," he said.

I drove to Warrenton and said good-bye to my grandmother. She knew none of the nuances of the military, the difference between a paratrooper and a guy slinging hash in some back-of-the-lines mess hall. All she knew was that she had already buried two sons because of the supposed "war to end all wars." And now her grandson was going to fight in another war. She hugged me and cried.

"If anything happens to you, Donnie Malarkey," she said, her eyes fixed on mine, "it'll be the end of me."

I headed back to our cabin in Cow Creek Valley. I walked along the Nehalem River and stared at the water and thought of all the old times: Bomba the Jungle Boy, fishing, camping.

It was nearly mid-September and the water was low; the heavy rains wouldn't begin for another couple of months. Fingerling salmon—sea-run cutthroat—darted here and there, soon off on their round-trip journeys to the Pacific Ocean thirty-five miles away. On the river bottom, the craw-dads were thick. I netted a few for later. A breeze roused the smell of blackberries, whose flavor had peaked weeks ago, but they still tasted sweet. At nightfall, I built a fire, steamed those crawdads, and had what you might call my own personal "last supper," washing my dinner down with a few bottles of Olympia beer.

Afterward, I stared at the embers deep into the night, trying, I suppose, to feel that sense of tranquillity I'd often felt out here as a kid, but I was never quite able to get there. It was as if I were being pulled toward something, some *place*— almost like these fingerling salmon that would instinctively swim to the sea each spring. Somehow, they just knew where they needed to be; just as, later on, they knew they needed to return to the river, the place where they'd started. Even if it meant swimming thirty-five miles upstream.

I slept back at the cabin. I left in the morning, before either my mother or father had awakened. I hadn't told them about my decision to become a paratrooper. But, like those salmon, I knew where I needed to be.

4

TOCCOA, SOBEL, AND SURVIVAL

Toccoa, Georgia
September–November 1942

I reported for duty in Portland and was sent, by train, to Fort Lewis with a group of about a hundred other inductees. It was September 12, 1942. We arrived at 4:00 A.M. and were told to report to an "indoctrination center." My buddy in Astoria had been right: As we sat in the room, among the first questions we were asked was whether any of us wanted to become paratroopers. Some of the guys didn't even know what the officer was talking about. What the hell was a paratrooper? Then he explained the concept, about jumping out of an airplane behind enemy lines, then fighting. About how it took a special man to volunteer. About how it took five jumps to earn your wings; and if you refused to jump, you could be court-martialed.

"If interested, please stand up," the officer said. Of the

hundred men, exactly two of us stood. Just down from me, still sitting, was a guy I'd known at the University of Oregon, Joe Montag.

"Well, so long, Malarkey," he said. "I'll never see *you* again."

Judging by the majority's choice, I figured I'd either gotten in with a group of really smart young men—or a bunch of namby-pamby chickens.

I was given a physical: five foot seven, 160 pounds. Good health. The other guy flunked his physical so it was just me heading to St. Louis, where I joined half a dozen other volunteers, including three who ultimately joined E Company, like me: Robert Rader, Don Hoobler, and William Howell. We were all on our way to a place called Toccoa, Georgia, where they'd separate the wheat from the chaff. The camp was located in the Chattahoochee National Forest, not far from a town called Toccoa, from which the camp got its name. It had been built specifically to form an experimental regiment that would feed into the Parachute School at Fort Benning, also in Georgia. About six thousand men were there. More than two out of three would either quit or be forced to quit. The rest would become paratroopers.

By the time I arrived, the regiment was pretty well formed and I was feeling a bit uneasy about fitting in. Newcomers were placed in W Company, a tented facility on the grassy slope of a hill just below the regimental medical-processing facility. We were a company in name only. The "W," I learned, stood for either "welcome" or "washout" because as we were coming, a group of guys were going. "This serves as the regiment's in-and-out processing machine," Burr Smith, a guy from southern California who'd been there a while, pointed out to me, "and it's a fast train in both directions."

For all my bravado back in Astoria, nobody here knew me

from Adam. From the get-go I feared my "W" might mean washout. Once assigned to E Company, I was having trouble just getting my cot put together; what made me think I could qualify for this elite group of soldiers? I'd already shown my inexperience by running into an officer I'd known back at the University of Oregon, Eugene Brown, and calling him Eugene instead of saluting him.

What's more, I'd heard that the group of guys leaving had been booted because of their inability to run up and and down something called Currahee.

"What's Currahee?" I asked one of them in my usual low, almost gravelly voice.

"Screw you, pal," said one them as he flung a duffel bag over his shoulder and headed out the door. Whatever it was, I guess he and it hadn't exactly hit it off.

That night, I would find out why. Currahee was a mountain, introduced to me by the first guy in E Company I became friends with. I was putting my shaving kit away on a shelf that had a photo of a young woman on it. I looked closer. Not only was she beautiful, but the name of the photo studio in the corner was familiar: WILSON STUDIO, ASTORIA, OREGON.

"Who's the photo of?" I asked a guy nearby.

"My sister."

"No kidding?" I said. "It was taken by Wilson Studio, in Astoria—where I'm from."

His eyes widened. "I'm from right across the Columbia in Ilwaco, Washington. Rod Bain's the name."

I was dumbfounded as we shook hands. Two thousand miles away and the guy bunking next to me was a ferry ride away from where I lived.

"Don Malarkey," I said.

"Welcome, and we're not the only Northwesterners: The

guy on the other side of my bunk is Tom Burgess. He's from Centralia, Washington. And John Plesha's from Seattle. Rainier Valley. So, Malarkey, after dinner, how 'bout a run up Currahee so you can understand what you'll be up against at Camp Toccoa?"

That night, after dinner, we walked to the foot of the mountain. Burgess joined us. "Currahee," said Bain, "is the measuring stick for us all. Quitting is a no-no. You quit and you qualify for 'moonlight patrol.'"

"Moonlight patrol?"

"Yeah, you quit Currahee and the next night you're sleeping away, dreaming of Lana Turner or your girl back home, and you get a tap on your shoulder. It's time for a command performance up the mountain. You and a bunch of other quitters—under the watchful eye of some noncom who's already cranky because he's having to babysit a bunch of wimps in the middle of the night."

If it was Bain's intention to scare me, it worked. It didn't help when, after a half mile up the three-mile-long logging road twisting through the pines, he and Burgess were gliding along and I was sucking eggs. Near the top, I thought I was going to lose my dinner. On the way down I thought I was going to lose everything I'd eaten since high school. It took about two hours, but, wheezing like an aging outboard motor, I made it.

At the bottom of the hill, Bain slapped me on the back in congratulation. As we bent over to catch our breath, he explained that "Currahee" was an Indian word that meant "standing alone."

"The battle cry of the 506th," he said, "is 'We stand alone together.'" He lowered his voice a notch for dramatic effect. "Currahee!" he yelled.

"Currahee!" followed Burgess.

Sweat had matted down my curly blond hair. I was bent over, my hands on my knees, trying to catch my breath, sweat dripping off my face. But hearing Burgess, I straightened up and, feeling like I'd somehow earned some tiny rite of passage, shouted my first battle cry.

"Currahee!"

That night, lying in my bunk, I wasn't thinking about being far away from Oregon or about how tired I was or about how a single mosquito—and there were squadrons of them at Toccoa—could spoil a night's sleep. Instead, I was thinking, what kind of a special group of guys was this that a couple of them—guys who didn't even know me—would run up a mountain just for my benefit? To help prepare me for what was to come? To welcome me in instead of trying to trample me down? It might have seemed a simple thing, but I've never forgotten that gesture. It was the first bonding experience with a group of men who would one day become known as the "band of brothers."

The "band of brothers," as we'd become known as after Stephen Ambrose's 1992 book of the same name, comes from Shakespeare's *Henry V,* 1598:

> We few, we happy few, we band of brothers;
> For he to-day that sheds his blood with me
> Shall be my brother.

Specifically, that label was given those of us in E, or Easy Company—decades after the war was over. The 101st Airborne Division, otherwise known as the Screaming Eagles, began in 1942. The 82nd Airborne had been the first of its kind to train men in assault from the air. We were next. Maj. Gen. William C. Lee promised us that although the 101st had no history, we had a "rendezvous with destiny." And a helluva rendezvous it would be.

Our 506th Parachute Infantry Regiment was one of three such regiments in the 101st, the others being the 501st and the 502nd. Each regiment had three battalions: A, B, and C companies were assigned to the 1st Battalion; D, E—that was us, Easy Company—and F assigned to the 2nd; and G, H, and I assigned to the 3rd. Easy Company, about 150 men strong, was divided into four platoons of 40 to 50 men each. I was in Easy's 2nd Platoon.

For Easy Company, virtually everything was at first some physical challenge: run Currahee three or four times a week; run a hillside obstacle course; over a stack of timber; under netting strewn with hog guts; through wooden chutes that left splinters in your hands; push-ups; sit-ups; windmills; somersaults; and do a forced march on Friday nights, starting out at five miles and adding five miles each week until the grand finale—a fifty-miler. No talking, no smoking— tough, since nearly all of us smoked like chimneys—no food, no water, and no stopping. Other companies didn't require such strictness. Other companies didn't have ambulances following them on their forced marches.

Then, I soon realized, E Company, 506th Parachute Infantry Regiment of the 101st Airborne Division, wasn't like "other companies." That's mainly because we were led by Capt. Herbert Sobel, the man who demanded the fifty-milers, the hog-guts-in-your-face obstacle courses, and the no-blinking-on-a-run-or-I'll-kick-your-ass rule on the Currahee runs.

"The men of Easy Company do not quit," he'd yell on our way up that mountain. "Do you understand me?"

At times, he'd have officers sweep through the ranks—guys like Lt. Dick Winters, who always obeyed Sobel's orders but wasn't totally sold on the man—checking our musette bags and canteens for food and water. Sobel had it in for Winters—was tougher than nails on him, almost as if Winters were one of "us" instead of one of "them."

After a week of sheer hell, Sobel would announce that we were being rewarded with a big dinner. You'd be halfway through your spaghetti when he'd walk in. We'd all snap to attention, and he'd say, "Gear on. We're going up Currahee. Now! Heigh-ho, Silver!"

Even in our "down" time, Sobel would find ways to make us miserable.

"Sobel reminds me of that joke about the captain of the slave galley," I told Skip Muck, a kid from New York I'd met, one afternoon as we were shining boots in the barracks. "First mate tells the guys who're rowing, 'Got good news and bad news for you, fellas. Good news is we're taking a day off tomorrow. Bad news is the captain wants to go waterskiing.'"

"You got that right, Malark," Skip said.

E Company inspections were legendary at Toccoa. Sobel would call them at any odd hour, bursting into the barracks with the surprise of some sneaker wave back home that'd sweep a fisherman right into the surf. Two weeks later, some crabber'd think he'd gotten the catch of a lifetime, pull up his ring, and find a body crawling with Dungeness crabs. At Toccoa, guys would disappear just like that, never to be heard of again. Couldn't cut it. Couldn't cut Sobel. Maybe both. One of them was a guy Skip and I knew, Bill Dickerson, from

Tacoma, Washington. Nice guy. I remember mugging for a photo with Skip and me in a doorway, pretending we were going to jump out of a plane. That's the closest Dickerson would get to jumping from a plane, though. Soon he, like dozens of others, was washed out to sea. Just like that.

Once, Sobel paid a surprise visit and confiscated all sorts of personal property from guys, everything from unauthorized ammo to a lifetime supply of rubbers to a can of peaches. Guys who'd disliked him before that incident hated him after it.

"Like to kill that SOB," you'd hear some guy mutter, "and I ain't kiddin'."

Sobel would look you eye to eye—he was tall—and start sneering at you and raising his voice just enough so you wanted to start choking him. "Dirt on your rifle's hinge spring, Malarkey. Weekend pass revoked."

Lint on your chevrons. *Revoked.* A rusty bayonet. *Revoked.* Don't like the sound of your name. *Revoked.* Sometimes, when one or two people had screwed up, he'd punish the whole bunch. There'd be some big dance we were all going to in town. *Sorry. No passes.* It was as if he were just trying to get our goat. Or maybe it was something deeper meant to make a bunch of misfits into a single unit.

He loved to humiliate us—or seemed to. Sometimes, as punishment, he'd make a guy sleep with a machine gun. Or go dig a six-foot-by-six-foot hole in the ground, then fill it back in. Jimmy Alley was always digging holes. When inspecting our 2nd Platoon, Sobel would come up to this kid named Frederick Belke. Seventeen years old. Never shaved in his life. Didn't need to; all he had was peach fuzz. Sobel would announce to the whole platoon that Belke was restricted for being unshaven so we all were restricted. Finally, we practically tied the kid down and shaved him ourselves.

Some called Sobel the Black Swan because he was dark-complected and ran like a duck, legs flapping here and there, but I admit, *he* did what *we* did. He'd get to the top of that mountain—frankly, not easy for him, but he'd never quit—with a stopwatch in his hand. "This might be good enough for the rest of the 506th, but it's sure as hell not good enough for Easy Company!"

In a strange way, it kind of filled you with pride. You got the idea he was hardening us for tougher times to come. That he truly wanted us to be the best of the bunch—and believed we could be. We wrestled, boxed, did decathlon events—and ran, ran, ran. Soon we established the finest fitness record in the 506th, but when some colonel from elsewhere saw the results, he couldn't believe it. So they sent this high muckety-muck from Washington, D.C., to retest us. We got an even higher score.

We were becoming exactly what Sobel wanted us to be: the best. But just when you were full of that pride—not that he ever told us he was proud of us—he'd find a way to suck it right out of you because you were so friggin' mad at him. You also felt you'd let him, and everyone else, down. You could never tell whether he wanted us to succeed or fail. Was his job to make us great soldiers or drum us out of the army in shame?

"The guy's the devil in jump boots," Muck said to me once, blowing smoke from a Lucky Strike skyward.

I couldn't disagree. By the time I left Toccoa, I wanted to tie Sobel to a loblolly pine and use him for slingshot practice. In the months to come, things would happen in training that would make a lot of us wonder if he were not only the devil in jump boots, but was going to get us killed in combat someday. When the war ended, I wondered something else about Herbert Sobel: I wondered if he wasn't a big reason some of us were still alive.

We were a bunch of guys in our early twenties from all over the country: gritty city boys like Guarnere, Southern boys such as Jimmy Alley, a few West Coasters—and everything in between. We'd been born soon after our fathers and uncles had gotten back—or been buried in Europe—after World War I. Had been hardened by a Depression that left some of our families bruised and battered. And inspired, after Pearl Harbor, to roll up our sleeves and serve our country—or at least go find some adventure in some place other than our hometowns. Only a few were married: Frank Perconte, Carwood Lipton, and a guy who'd join us at Fort Bragg, Alton More, come to mind. Most of us were young, single, and, too often, stupid, but as the weeks wore on, we started to bond.

I found myself surrounded by all sorts of guys who came to be my friends. Bain, of course, was the first guy I'd met, and growing up on the Columbia, he knew the difference between a chinook and a sockeye salmon. As a native Northwesterner, I appreciated that. Jimmy Alley, a kid from Arkansas, wanted me to believe that grits were actually food; guys like him had no idea how wonderful a crab cocktail or razor clams tasted. Alley was a bundle of energy, but it was sometimes like the energy of a firecracker—prone to blow up in his face. Sobel was always giving him extra duty for this or that.

Joe Toye, from Pittston, Pennsylvania, was Irish like me but far stronger; he was like sprung steel. Toughest guy in the unit, bar none, even if that brute strength seemed to hide some wounds deep inside. Bill Guarnere arrived with excellent combative credentials, being from South Philly—and with an accent to match. Don Moone, a private in the 3rd Platoon, had a brain that worked on the same wavelength as mine. Good man. Then there was Sal Bellino, a Brooklyn kid with a great singing voice; Ed "Step-and-a-Half" Stein, whose gait was about half again as much as mine; and Father John Maloney, the 506th chaplain, a guy who would somehow find a way to ground us to the deeper things, amid the grit of war. There were others—John Sheehy, Eugene Jackson, Herman Hansen, Earl "One Lung" McLung, Chuck Grant—whom I called my friends. Great guys all.

But of all the men I'd come to know at Toccoa, my closest pal quickly became Skip Muck. Every platoon—about forty-five guys—had four squads that consisted of three rifle squads and a six-man mortar squad. Along with Skip, I was assigned to a mortar squad as a gunner. We were a team, Skip and I. I'd sight. He'd drop the rounds down the tube. We bunked in the same barracks, and when we'd run Currahee, we usually wound up side by side.

"How ya feeling?" he'd ask.

"Like I'd rather be cleaning barnacles off the bottom of a trawler."

Which is about as much as we'd get in before Sobel and his eagle eyes would catch our lips moving and bust us with fifty push-ups. "Catch up to the rest before we reach the top, dammit, or you'll be scrubbing toilets," he'd say.

On the run that Sobel surprised us with in the middle of dinner, Skip, like a handful of others, started puking about two-thirds of the way up. He stopped and bent over.

"The men of Easy Company do not quit!" Sobel shouted, his eyes boring down on Skip. "Do you understand me?"

Instinctively, I grabbed Skip's arm to keep him going. "Skip, com'n, pal, you can do this. *We* can do this. No quitting." He wiped his face with his white paratrooper's undershirt, nodded slightly, and continued on.

Warren H. Muck was about the millionth kid our age to be named after Warren Harding, a fairly popular president from 1921 to 1923, when a lot of us World War II kids were being born. No wonder he preferred "Skip."

We were different in some ways. We couldn't have grown up farther apart—Oregon and New York. He was from Tonawanda, just north of Buffalo and along the Niagara River. My roots were Irish, his German; he even spoke a fair amount of it. When it came to drinking and gambling, I was a major leaguer while Skip was happy to bounce around the minors, playing here and there, but the more we got to know each other, the more we realized we had lots in common.

We both had that adventurous spirit; while I was swinging across ravines on the branches of Douglas firs in Oregon's woods, Skip was swimming across the Niagara River in New York. We were both about five-seven or five-eight, he a bit more wiry. We were both a little ornery, mischievous, and athletic; he played wide receiver in football and was on the swim team.

Both of us liked a good laugh. Both of us were nuts for music: Glenn Miller, Benny Goodman, Harry James, The Mills Brothers singing "Paper Doll," and Frank Sinatra's "Moonlight Serenade." At the end of a day, we'd go to the PX—it wasn't much bigger than a boxcar—and were usually so tired that we'd sit on the floor, our backs to the wall, and with a beer or Coke in our hands listen to that jukebox until I thought we were going to wear out the grooves in those

78 rpm records. It wasn't just the sound of the music, it was what it could do to you inside: take you away from endless days of sweating, grunting, and cussing beneath your breath at Sobel.

Skip and I both had girlfriends back home. OK, Skip had a girlfriend and I *sort of* had a girlfriend. I'd broken things off with Bernice back in college, but away from home, I missed her terribly and we began exchanging letters again. She'd gone to summer music school at Mills College, then to New York City to be a professional singer. Skip's girlfriend was Faye Tanner, a cheerleader he'd met from another high school in the place he grew up. The more we talked about our girls, the more we realized that even they were similar. Pretty. Catholic. Loyal—Bernice even when I didn't deserve it. Their letters picked us up on many a Toccoa day.

The Depression had been hard on both our families. In some ways, we both were forced to become the "man of the house." My dad essentially bailed out in 1938; his dad abandoned his family in about 1930, deciding he'd rather play in a jazz band and travel the country than be a father. Beyond that, we both were happy-go-lucky, witty, a little nutty, prickly when provoked, and, here and there, prone to laugh in the face of the odds if we thought, after doing so, we'd survive to live another day. How else do you explain our trying to become paratroopers? How else do you explain a guy swimming the Niagara? Or me defying an ROTC colonel?

Skip was the real deal; didn't have a phony bone in his body. Unassuming and yet had a personality that drew people to him like cold hands to a fire. He was the barracks peacekeeper on occasion. Not the guy who demanded to be in the spotlight but probably the best-liked man in the company. A guy who could make each of us feel as if he were his best friend. Deep down, I felt honored that he even had time for a maverick like me.

Others soon realized we were best buddies. Burr Smith, an Easy Company soldier who'd been to a private military school in southern California, would write this about Muck and me when the war was over:

Warren "Skippy" Muck [was] an upstate New Yorker of great charm and wit who drew people to him like a magnet. Quiet, unassuming, totally "real," his strength was revealed in combat, where his 2d Platoon mortar section earned a fearsome reputation as Easy Company's most effective heavy weapons element. Skippy was a happy guy, and those who knew him basked in the warmth of that happiness and were happy, too. His closest friend, and, inevitably one of mine, was Don Malarkey, another warm, friendly and happy-go-lucky individual who likewise rose to the top of my list of personal heroes like cream to the top of the old-fashioned glass milk bottle.

In some ways, Skip had replaced my family and my pals at the Sigma Nu house as the person I was closest to on earth. Once, on our way back to the barracks from the PX, Skip and I were having a smoke when he asked me why I chose airborne. I told him about growing up with the stories about my uncles both giving their lives for their country.

"I dunno, Skip, I think I was just born to do this," I said.

His response didn't surprise me in the least: "Me, too, Malark."

But we never talked about *not* making it home. We only talked about what it would be like when we *did*, how we'd visit each other and he'd show me where he'd swum the Niagara and I'd take him fishing on the Nehalem, maybe out in the ocean for salmon.

"Going out over the Columbia River bar makes swimming the Niagara look like kiddy stuff," I huffed.

"We'll do it," he said. "But, remember, I swam the Niagara at *night*."

5

SKIP MUCK AND THE MARCH TO ATLANTA

Toccoa, Benning, Mackall, and Bragg
November 1942 to September 1943

By November 1942, Easy Company was becoming a finely tuned company—even if, for the second time, I'd run into Eugene Brown, my old University of Oregon classmate, and called him Eugene instead of showing him the proper respect as an officer. We'd done a fifty-mile Friday-night march through the Chattahoochee National Forest where you couldn't eat, drink, talk, or smoke; you just put your head down and went. It may have been the most difficult thing we did. But those were the things that drew us together, like we were one unit instead of a hundred-plus guys.

We hadn't jumped yet, our practice limited to jumping from thirty-foot towers in parachute harnesses suspended by steel cables, but we were prepared to take on anything on the ground. So our West Point colonel, William Sink, decided to try just that. Someone had shown him a *Reader's Digest* article that said a Japanese army battalion had set a world record by marching a hundred miles in seventy-two hours. Sink decided we'd do the Japanese one better. He ordered his best battalion, the 2nd, to do a forced march from Toccoa southwest to Atlanta. More than one hundred men marching 118 miles. Under Sobel's orders, we were not to cross roads when we stopped for breaks. And the real killer: We were to do all this with full field equipment.

That was bad enough for regular guys carrying guns, especially the guys like Walter Gordon who had machine guns. But for mortarmen, like Skip and me, it was like being asked to climb Mount Everest with a pack full of bricks on our backs. The parts of a mortar unit weighed sixty-five pounds. Still, the challenge was intriguing, as if our team were finally getting in a game to see what we were made of.

It was late November. We marched about forty-five miles the first day in wind, rain, and cold. I felt good. The second day, hail and sleet joined the mix. My legs started giving me trouble from the constant pounding on concrete; the sixty-five-pound mortar seemed to double in weight. I was dying of thirst.

About noon, we were taking a break when a woman in front of a farmhouse, across a road, asked if we could use some water. I looked around. Lieutenant Winters was up at the head of the formation. I couldn't see Sobel, so I told my squad leader, Bill Guarnere, that I was going for it. I ran across the road and filled two canteens for me and the guys. Suddenly, I saw him down the road, heading my way like a Labrador to a downed bird—Sobel.

"I want that man's name!" he shouted, a finger pointing my way.

Just then, though, the column started moving forward and Sobel's path to me was blocked by marching soldiers. I scampered back across the road and into the mass of olive drab, having dodged a dangerous bullet. Skip was proud. But over the last day and a half my legs had gotten progressively worse and I barely made that evening's destination, Oglethorpe University, on Atlanta's outskirts.

Skip put up our pup tents and I lay down to rest. In the distance, I could hear Joe Toye singing some Irish song that had been passed down from his folks. At chow call, I couldn't even stand up. I started to literally crawl on my hands and knees through the woods to the chow line. Skip stopped me, grabbed my mess kit, and said, "No friend of mine crawls anywhere." He filled both our plates and came back to eat with me. After dinner, I just sat there, my mind numb, my legs on fire.

"My shins are killin' me, Skip. I don't know if I can make it."

"Almost there, buddy. Only thirty-eight miles."

"*Only* thirty-eight?"

"Eighty down. You can do this, Malark. *We* can do this."

"I dunno, Skip."

"I'll get you to Atlanta if I have to drag you."

Later, Lieutenant Winters came to see me in the tent. He figured I had severe shin splints.

"Why don't you plan on going the rest of the way in a rig, Malarkey."

"Sir, give me a night's rest," I said, glancing at Skip. "I think I can make it."

Winters paused, then shook his head sideways. "Whatever you think."

I made Atlanta. We all made Atlanta—seventy-five hours

from the time we started. As we marched down Peachtree Street to Five Corners in Atlanta, a few national radio networks announced to the world what we had done—beat the Japanese record, and beat it good. Afterward, my legs were terribly swollen. I spent three days in bed. But I'd made it. That's partly because when we got close to Atlanta, we were joined by either a military or university band that led us; that music inspired me. And partly because to quit was to be like someone back home whom I didn't want to be like. And partly because Skip Muck was in my ear the whole time, telling me I was going to make it if he had to throw me over his shoulder.

Fort Benning, about a hundred miles southwest of Atlanta, was the next stop in our journey to become paratroopers. We hadn't been there long when the sizing-up began. We were coming out of the mess hall when some 82nd Airborne paratroopers spotted us. They looked us up and down with their arms crossed and a few head-nodding smirks.

"So, here come the long-walking, loud-talking, non-*jumping* 'sonobitches' 506ers," said one.

I'll bet everyone in Easy Company wanted to lunge at those guys with fists flying, but by now, thanks to Sobel, we'd actually learned a touch of discipline. And in some ways, who could blame them for having their shorts in a bunch? Though these guys hadn't seen action, they'd at least jumped out of planes. And some in the 82nd had already fought in North Africa and Sicily. Here at Benning, these guys had heard about our fitness records. Read all the headlines about the world-record march. Heard the stories of our forced marches, the nighttime assaults on Currahee. But we were newbies at Benning and, to this point, hadn't done anything more than jump out of a parachute tower, harnessed to a cable, and land in a pile of straw. In their eyes, we were over-hyped rookies who hadn't proven a damn thing.

Benning was our chance to change that. Earning your wings as a paratrooper required four steps: The A stage was physical fitness; B involved practice work on the parachute towers and learning landing techniques, some of which we got at Toccoa; C was learning to pack your own chutes (and unpack . . . and repack, etc.); D was the final week at Benning, when you made your five required jumps.

A and D were the trapdoors for the guys who weren't going to cut it. Though we'd gained a few newcomers, we'd lost dozens of guys who just couldn't manage the physical part of the training. We knew who had lungs and legs. Now, aboard C-47s heading into the skies over Georgia, we were going to find out who had balls. To refuse to jump, even once, was to be bounced from the Airborne. If a guy froze in practice, how the hell could you trust that he was going to jump when the enemy was waiting below?

My worst thought was having to send a letter home saying I'd washed out. I'd be betraying the memory of my two uncles by failing. So, no, I couldn't fail, I thought as we sat, nine to either side of the lumbering two-engine aircraft. We were wearing some team's old football helmets, a scene that probably wouldn't have scared the hell out of the krauts. Nerves were taut. This was it: time for our first jump, though I can honestly say I wasn't scared. Just anxious.

"Stand up and hook up!" the jumpmaster yelled over the thrum of the engines.

You could barely hear him.

"Check equipment!"

I checked mine. I checked the man in front of me.

"Sound off!" The last man in the "stick"—the name given to a group of parachutists—yelled, "Eighteen, OK!" and slapped the guy ahead of him on the back. "Seventeen, OK!" "Sixteen, OK." "Fifteen, OK!" "Fourteen—"

Suddenly, a guy in front of me panicked and grabbed a parallel support bar on the fuselage of the plane. Those of us who were behind him had to unhook our chutes and re-hook on the other side of him. Later, I learned that it had taken four people from the parachute school to pull him from the plane after it had landed. He was immediately whisked off to the guardhouse. We saw him a few days later at a special battalion ceremony that's still seared into my mind.

It was a "drumming out" ceremony in honor— make that dishonor —of those who couldn't cut it. As hundreds of us watched—were forced to watch—they were stripped of patches from their caps and the 506th patch from their arms. A jeep drove up and dumped each guy's barracks bag, and, with tommy guns at their backs, they were marched away, no longer paratroopers but infantrymen. Frankly, it was sickening, not the proudest day in American military history. Had word got back to Washington, D.C., about this, some heads would have rolled. But the mournful drums kept beating as the men were marched onto the reviewing area, publicly humiliated.

Back in the plane, the jumpmaster was yelling, "Go! Go!"

The line got shorter, my stomach churned harder, part of me scared, but most of me knowing that this was what all the hard work came down to: to step into the unknown with a bunch of other guys who were just as scared as I was but were still willing to leap.

Remember what you've learned, Malarkey: Keep your fingers outside the door. Don't look down. Watch the horizon—and the other guys' chutes, to make sure you're heading down at the same rate.

The jumpmaster looked at me. The light on the inside of the aircraft turned from red to green. "Go!"

I jumped. With the cover of my chute attached to the static line, the chute itself would open on its own. I remembered to count to four out loud: *One thousand one.* I heard the crackling of the canopy over my head as the prop blast caught it. *One thousand two.* The connector links whistled past. I clung to the reserve chute on my chest. *One thousand three.* I felt like a rag doll, falling at more than a hundred miles per hour. I held my breath. *One thousand four.* The wind rippled my face, far worse than any gale-force storm I'd experienced on Oregon's windy north coast.

Then, boom, I felt a tug. The canopy had opened. *Breathe.* The ground in front of me stopped swaying quite as much as it initially had. I opened the risers to help the chute fully open, then looked up. *Whew. No blown panels.* Looking around, I realized I was floating down at the same rate as the others, a comforting sign that nothing was out of whack.

The field below was coming at me fast. I pulled on my risers for positioning. Noticed an ambulance to my left. *Gulp.* Then, closer, closer, closer. I turn back into the wind. And then, boots on the ground, a quick jolt of pain, and swirling around like the parachute I was trying to gather in, the fleeting thought that that was a helluva lot farther to fall than from the roof of our house back home.

Later that week, I completed my second and third jumps. Two more and I was home free. "Sound off!" yelled the jumpmaster on our fourth attempt. There was only one problem: I'd contracted a bad cold and had laryngitis. Could barely get a word out, so I'd quickly asked the guy in front of me to shout my number. He did so, but the jump master knew something was amiss and came back to see me. I had described the problem on a piece of cardboard, which I flashed at him. Convinced I was willing and able, he didn't pull me from the stick.

I successfully completed that jump, then came the all-important fifth. "Go!" I flew into the air. When my boots hit the ground, it was sweet relief. I'd earned my wings. I was a U.S. army paratrooper. After the ceremony, at a party in our honor, we threw back more than a few beers. It had been four months since I'd arrived at Toccoa, wondering if that "W" would stand for "welcome" or "washout." Now I knew. And Skip had made it, too.

Wings Day was one of proudest days of my life. Not only was I proud of myself, but of every man in Easy Company, period. A few weeks later, the unit publication of the 504th Parachute Regiment of the 82nd Airborne Division—called *Static Line*—encouraged its personnel to show a bit more respect to the 506th. At Benning, the 82nd's 505th and 507th regiments had gone through school with a 21.06 percent washout rate. Ours was 1.53.

Beyond the pride, the wings meant $50 more pay per month. Each month, I would send my mother my $50 jump pay and $15 of my regular pay, with instructions that it was not to be saved for me but to be used for her and dad and my sister. It seemed a meager amount, but out in the cabin, their expenses weren't huge. My mother cooked over a woodstove that also heated the cabin.

I hoped those checks I sent home were somehow reassuring to my mother, and deep down I hoped they might ease the guilt I felt from pressing on to be a paratrooper against her will. I'm not sure what they meant to my father, if anything.

It was a routine jump. Spring 1943, and we were at our next training stop, Camp Mackall in North Carolina, not far from Fort Bragg. My stick went out over a small lake, the wind blowing enough to nudge jumpers clear of the water. When my chute opened, I followed the split-second protocol of looking at the other guys' chutes to make sure I was descending at the same rate. For the first time ever, that wasn't the case. The other chutes seemed to be going up, which obviously meant I was going down way too fast. Something was wrong. Very wrong.

I looked up at my canopy. *Oh my God!* I had about five blown panels—of the twenty-four total—and five dangling suspension lines. Without much air in the canopy, I was falling like a rock, near the edge of a lake. I reached for my reserve chute but made a major blunder. *Always throw it out in the opposite direction that you're oscillating.* Instead, I pulled the bonehead stunt of throwing it out the *same* way I was turning. It slowed me, but in a split second, I was engulfed in my reserve chute and couldn't see anything.

In seconds, I was crashing through the leaves and limbs of an oak tree. My suspension lines went taut just before I was going to hit the ground, and I just hung there, bouncing a bit as if on a swing. My chute was draped over the tree. Later, I figured out I'd done a Mickey Mouse job of packing my chute. I'd accidentally packed a "shot bag" with my chute— a tube of BBs about eighteen inches long that we'd use to smooth out each panel. The BBs must have broken free and punctured the panels. Fortunately, it was the last time I'd be required to pack my own chute; after ten jumps, that became someone else's responsibility.

At the time, I was too panicked to put the incident into perspective. Later, I realized how close I'd come to dying that day. Looking back, it's funny how the deeper into war you get, the more the danger becomes almost second nature. And the less you keep believing that you can keep dodging the bullet that has your name on it.

At Mackall, our training became more about weapons and strategy. More sophisticated. We still ran a lot, but the emphasis was now largely unit-oriented. Field problems. Night patrols. Communication between units. "What-if" challenges.

If soldiers, to this point, despised Sobel because of his attitude, now they started doubting his skills. He always wanted us to believe he was smarter than any other man in the company, but he was having trouble proving it. He would make a tactical error in some war game that led us straight into enemy hands. He would linger way too long over a simple map. Or make a decision, then suddenly change his mind.

"That SOB's gonna get us killed" wasn't an uncommon utterance in Easy Company. My thoughts: He was going to get *himself* killed. The only question was who was going to be pulling the trigger—the krauts or us.

Meanwhile, though, I'd realized there wasn't much I could do about who was leading us. All I could do was become the best damn soldier I could be and let the chips fall where they may. To that end, I won a three-day pass to Washington, D.C., for placing first in a weapons competition with the M1 rifle: who could dismantle and reassemble it fastest while blindfolded. I all but flunked the hand-to-hand combat training—Winters gave me a scolding—because I just couldn't visualize myself poking a bayonet in another man's chest. But I was good with rifles, having done some hunting as a kid.

From June until the end of the year, we bounced around: maneuvers in Kentucky (encountered copperhead snakes) and Tennessee (encountered chiggers, little bugs that burrow in your skin and had so deeply infiltrated my back that the army had me flown to a hospital at Fort Bragg, North Carolina). Bragg was where the 506th was headed anyway, so the others soon caught up to me.

Bragg was a plush hotel compared to the other camps we'd been at. Our preparation shifted to getting ready to go overseas. There were repeated inspections, vaccination shots we had to get, and equipment handouts, not to mention brawls at the Town Pump Tavern in nearby Fayetteville. Soldiers were getting anxious, the testosterone was thick, and the beer cold. A dangerous combination, especially given the number of paratroopers, known for their cockiness, at Bragg.

In July, ten months after I'd enlisted, E Company gathered for the company photograph. One hundred and seventeen men (a few dozen were no-shows for whatever reasons; 140 men formed the original company). Hands behind their backs, uniforms crisp, trousers bloused above the paratrooper boots. On one hand, ready for war. And yet, looking back, not ready in the least. You could never be totally ready for what you'd find in war.

It was summer 1943. Soon we'd be headed for New York and a trip to England. First, though, we got furloughs. At National Airport in Washington, D.C., flights were full, but a

Red Cross girl walked me to a counter and showed them my "priority" ticket. I was on the next flight west.

At this point, Bernice was back in New York to seek her fame and fortune as a singer; we'd split up again—my idea again—after I'd visited her on a leave and found she'd lost her athletic figure. It had been stupid of me to drop a girl because her dress size had gone up and I was without excuse.

When I arrived home, seeing my military uniform sent my already fragile mother into an emotional tailspin. To her, it said, *My baby's all grown-up.* It said, *Danger ahead.* Grandmother Malarkey was her saintly self, if not clutching her rosary tighter than usual. "I'll pray for you every day, Donnie," she said. But, like Mom, she found my return less comforting than worrisome; I had to keep reminding myself that she had two sons in Ocean View Cemetery because of war.

I said good-bye to my father, but I'm not sure if he even heard me; as usual, he was just sitting there, in his favorite chair, staring off into something the rest of us could never see. If we already were something of a fractured family, it would only get worse. My younger brother was struggling with anger. He'd soon be expelled from high school for coldcocking a coach with a right hook after a disagreement. At seventeen, he would become an underage enlistee in the navy.

I stayed a week. In a sense, I'd said my good-byes the year before. I had just turned twenty-two, and for some reason, this was almost harder, like ripping open a scab that was nearly healed. I'd just gotten over Grandma Malarkey's statement from a few months back—"If anything happens to you, it'll be the end of me"—and didn't want to go through it again.

On the trip back, on a United Airlines flight, I thought about the pleasant fires we had in the cabin's fireplace that burned the big alder logs. I had no idea how much I'd miss such simple comforts, let alone electric lights. In Chicago, because of a flight cancellation, I was delayed in returning to Fort Bragg. Even though I had written evidence of my delay, Sgt. William Evans threatened to court-martial me. It wouldn't be the last time.

In late August, the 506th boarded a train from North Carolina to New York, and on September 5, we set sail aboard the British ship *Samaria*. Five thousand men crammed onto an older passenger ship designed for less than half that. I stood on the upper deck as we churned out of New York Harbor and watched as we passed the Statue of Liberty. It was enough to put a lump in a guy's throat, wondering if you'd ever be back to see this country of yours again.

Back home, the hundreds of mothers with boys in Easy Company had been sent letters from Sobel that, for the first time, suggested the guy might actually have a heart.

Dear Madam,

Soon your son [each individual name had been typed in] will drop from the sky to engage and defeat the enemy. He will have the best of weapons, and equipment, and have had months of hard, and strenuous training to prepare him for success on the battlefield.

Your frequent letters of love, and encouragement, will arm him with a fighting heart. With that, he cannot fail, but will win glory for himself, make you proud of him, and his country ever grateful for his service in its hour of need.

He signed each letter, naturally not telling our families where we were headed. En route to England, all unit insignia was ordered removed from clothing to keep confidential that we were paratroopers; the less the Germans knew of our whereabouts before the invasion, someone figured, the better. However, before docking, the order was reversed and we sewed the patches back on, apparently to increase the morale of the British. Europe, we were reminded, had already been at war for four years, and even something small, like a patch of a screaming eagle, could let the British know they were no longer fighting this war alone.

Along with tens of thousands of other soldiers from the United States and elsewhere who were arriving here in England, we were to help end it.

6

PRELUDE TO THE GREAT CRUSADE

England
September 1943 to June 1944

While in England, the 2nd Battalion, of which Easy Company was part, made a demonstration jump before Winston Churchill, Dwight Eisenhower, and other high muckety-mucks. We assembled after the jump in front of the reviewing stand at Greenham Common Airbase, where General Maxwell Taylor invited dignitaries to inspect the ranks, and where, the day before D-day, "Ike" would make a more famous visit to the 502nd Regiment. For some reason, I was in the front rank rather than in the mortar squad's normal position toward the rear.

Ike and Churchill were going down the line, stopping and talking to about one person in each frontal squad. I have no idea how they chose each person, whether by count, by random, or by how impressively a soldier came to attention as the two dignitaries passed by. But before I knew it, the supreme commander of the Allied forces in Europe, the man responsible for planning and supervising the invasion of France and Germany, was suddenly saluting me, Don Malarkey, an ROTC dropout.

"Where you from, soldier?" Eisenhower said.

"Astoria, Oregon, *sir*."

For some reason, I wasn't as flustered by all this as you might imagine.

"And what were you doing before the war?"

"Going to school at the University of Oregon, sir."

"So, who won that Oregon–Oregon State football game last year?"

I told him I wasn't sure, though the truth is nobody won because all the players were off playing soldier.

"And what are your plans after the war, soldier?"

"Uh, return to school, sir."

"Well, good luck to you, young man," Ike said, shaking my hand.

He then asked if Churchill had any questions for me.

"Yes, how do you like England?" he asked. Photographers were snapping pictures. This, I quickly reminded myself, was the prime minister of Great Britain.

"Very much, sir. I enjoy the literature and the history in particular."

What I didn't tell him was that the dank, rainy, cloudy English weather made the northern Oregon coast feel like the Bahamas. That the food was horrible—all that mutton. That I once got a pancake so heavy and thick and undercooked that it weighed roughly as much as my mortar tube. At one point, two-thirds of our barracks had been hospitalized or confined to our beds because of sickness related to the food.

I liked the English countryside, and I wasn't lying when I said I liked the history and literature. I liked the people, in particular a bartender named Patrick McGrath. I marveled at the children, whose grammar, diction, and vocabulary was impressive. I liked the comfort of English trains and the expanse of Paddington Station. I liked lots of things about England, but the food and the weather balanced the scales.

Another thing I didn't like about England: the cheesy "photo op" we later got suckered into with the British general Bernard "Monty" Montgomery. The 2nd Battalion of the 506th had been secluded on a wooded British estate several hundred yards from his manor. At a prearranged signal, we were to run, arms upraised, toward the patio, where the general was in view. In the days that followed, newspapers depicted American paratroopers and glider men running toward Montgomery in adulation. In my book, it was bush-league stuff, plain and simple.

I enjoyed another "showcasing" much more. We were doing exercises on the south coast. Sgt. Bill Guarnere had me sight the mortar directly on a six-foot-square white target on a fore dune, about six hundred yards away. With Skip loading the mortars, I fired two rounds, one a little short, one a little long. Right after the second one hit, the "brass" arrived, a staff officer from division headquarters, accompanied by a general.

"Sergeant," the staff officer said to Guarnere, "have the gunners fire at that white target as a demonstration for the general. No sighting first."

Guarnere turned to us and half-winked. "Three rounds, men."

I looked at Skip. He looked at me. We were both thinking

the same thing—that, unbeknownst to our observers, we'd just adjusted our fire on that very target. The first round hit dead center. The other two landed right on top of the first.

The general's eyebrows raised in either respect or disbelief. "Sergeant," he said, "is your squad always this accurate?"

With his best South Philly cockiness, Guarnere took great pleasure in replying, "Sir, my squad never misses. *Never.*"

Skip Muck's smile that day was like a sideways banana. It would be one of my best memories of him. Soon after, I was called in to see Lt. Dick Winters.

"Private Malarkey, I'm splitting up you and Skip."

"Sir?"

"You both are on a trajectory to being noncommissioned officers. Makes no sense, then, to keep you in the same platoon. Skip's going to the First, you'll stay in the Second."

Though disappointed, the news didn't devastate me. Hell, I couldn't argue with the reasoning; much as I had little passion for leadership, it appeared I was headed in that direction, as was Skip. But I'm not sure Winters gave me the straight dope. Later, I heard he had other reasons for splitting us up. He told some that Muck and Malarkey were like brothers; if one gets killed or wounded, the other'll be worthless. And the invasion was fast approaching.

We were quartered in the village of Aldbourne, in south England, about a hundred miles west of London. We stayed in both wood and Quonset-type buildings with a potbelly stove in each and toilets outside. We called them honey pots. They stunk to high heaven. I don't know what was worse, that smell, the food, or Joe Toye missing a note on one of his late-night Irish songs. I fancied myself a fairly decent singer, so noticed those missed notes. Let's just say Joe was a far better soldier than singer.

Our training reverted back to a Toccoa-type schedule with a heavy accent on running, calisthenics, and forced marches. At first, we were working six days a week, so weekend passes were out. But that would change. Meanwhile, we found ourselves, unlike back in the States, part of a larger community of people instead of out in the middle of nowhere. Occasionally, we'd visit one of the several pubs in Aldbourne. I became a crack dart player and seldom had to buy a beer. Beyond darts, I'd emerged as one of the best poker and dice players in Easy Company; I guess that was some sort of extension of my days in Astoria as a hot marbles player. Gram Malarkey sent me cigarettes and candy. Other than getting humiliated by Joe Toye in a friendly wrestling match—he batted me around like I was a popcorn ball—things were going well.

One day, Winters came to me. "Malarkey," he said, "I want to make you a noncom, but you've got to show more initiative."

"Like what?" I asked, wondering why he'd want to make me a noncommissioned officer.

"Throwing a few orders at your fellow privates, try to get them to be more dedicated."

I told him I couldn't do that; it just wasn't my style. "I'll gladly serve you in combat," I told him. But, no, I wasn't going to act like some kind of Boy Scout just to impress him. It wasn't a matter of me not "walking the talk," because I'd never talked about wanting to be a leader. I didn't need fancy stripes on my sleeves, just a parachute and a rifle. I don't think my answer thrilled Winters, but I think he appreciated my honesty and knew I'd come around.

In England, the idea of war started becoming more real than it was back in the States. We started hearing the people's stories of the bombings in London; even in the rural areas, where people weren't huddling in subways, the British people were weary. Few young men were in the villages; most were off fighting the Germans or Japanese.

Our first opportunity for a weekend pass meant one thing to me: London. Everywhere you looked, you'd see soldiers from all different countries: Canada, South Africa, New Zealand. And with the British boys all off fighting, women galore. We stayed in the Regent Palace Hotel.

One Saturday afternoon, Joe Toye and I wandered into a place on Charing Cross Road called the Palace Pub. Joe was from Pennsylvania; I thought it was the perfect fit because the guy was like Pittsburgh-made steel. He'd gotten strong because of working in the coal mines. He didn't have a huge vocabulary, but had this wonderful Irish brogue—didn't hear that much in Oregon—and he came across like Super-man, a guy who had all this strength but never let it go to his head.

But after a few beers that day, I saw another side of Joe Toye.

"My mother and father both grew up in Ireland, then came to America," he told me that day. "When I was a kid, my father says to me, 'Joey. You're Irish. You have two choices. You work in the coal mines or you be a cop. That's it.'"

" 'That's it'?" I said.

" 'That's it. You're too young to be a cop, so it's off to the mines.' I remember the priest coming to talk to him about me going back to school. He shooed him away. I was a coal miner. That was that."

He paused. "I was fifteen, Malark. *Fifteen.*"

"Same age I was when I worked the salmon nets on the Columbia."

"Only you still got to go to school. I had to quit. Football coaches were drooling over me but I couldn't play. I never learned to write. Never learned to talk good like you guys can with the big words and stuff. . . ." His words trailed off and he stared at his beer.

I didn't know what to say. But I remember thinking what a great guy Joe Toye was. We just went on drinking beer, then got onto other topics and finally started looking around the pub and noticing all the framed, autographed pictures on the high-ceilinged walls. After a couple of beers, I asked the barkeep the significance of the pictures.

He said he'd been the captain of a British soccer team that had toured the United States in 1929 and 1930—and had made lots of American friends because of it.

"Pat McGrath's the name," he said, extending his hand.

"Must have been a helluva player," I said, shaking his hand. "An Irishman captaining a British soccer team?"

Pat McGrath and I became close friends in the months before the invasion. I liked him a lot—and his pub, too. Twenty-foot-high ceilings. Autographed pictures on the walls of Mary Pickford and Douglas Fairbanks. He talked of moving to America after the war; his cousin was Jimmy Walker, the mayor of New York, and he thought Mr. Walker might help get him established. When "afternoon closing" came—British law said pubs had to be closed between 3:00 P.M. and 6:00 P.M.—the patrons would leave, but Pat would keep me and my buddies on as his personal guests. One night, I finished off a beer and extended my hand to Pat McGrath. "Until we meet again, my friend," I said.

Among the many painful ironies of war, I would soon

learn, is that though it's fought by soldiers, civilians get caught in the cross fire. Which is why that was the last time I would see Pat McGrath.

England became a double-edged sword for Easy Company. One edge was the privilege of weekend passes to London or wherever you wanted to roam in the countryside. Easy Company did nothing to disprove the reputation of paratroopers as first-class hell-raisers. We were all in our early twenties and had never had such freedom, such opportunities. For some, that meant god-awful hangovers, cases of the clap from the always available women of the night, and a month's wages lost on the poker table. I confess, I let some of my youthful energy carry me away on occasion; after a particularly lively pub experience, Rod Bain told me the next morning that I'd recited every line of Kipling's "Gunga Din"—while standing atop the bar. No wonder my jump boots smelled like stale beer.

The other edge of the sword was more worrisome. Under Captain Sobel, company morale was sinking like a torpedoed sub. We were adding some new officers; given the potential for losing men, the goal was two lieutenants per platoon. Among the newcomers was a guy named Lynn "Buck" Compton, a star catcher on the UCLA baseball team and a football player as well. In fact, as a guard, he'd blocked for Jackie Robinson on UCLA's 1942–43 Rose Bowl team. He was warm. Friendly. And he would become a good friend of mine. He knew of a number of players from the University of Oregon's football and basketball teams, guys I'd gone to college with. In fact, he would become a good friend of lots of guys, which would cause some friction with Winters, who thought officers shouldn't be playing poker with the enlisted men. Compton was forever sneaking out and playing cards with the guys, though he'll swear he only did it once or twice. Frankly, like Buck, I thought the line between officers and enlisted men was drawn far too deep in the ground; hell, we were all going off to fight the same war. But that would be small-time friction compared to the cold war of Captain Sobel and Lieutenant Winters that came to a head in the fall of 1943.

Sobel was bearing down on us—and on the officers and noncoms—like never before. Frankly, I think the guy was scared stiff. One night, he totally screwed up on a simple maneuver. His own men played a trick on him when he encountered a barbed-wire fence: From behind some bushes, Pvt. George Luz—a Portuguese jokester and master of imitation—yelled at Sobel to cut through a barbed-wire fence while the rest of us tried to muffle our laughter. When Sobel questioned the command, Luz identified himself as "Major Oliver Horton," the battalion executive officer. Damned if Sobel didn't cut the fence—and later caught hell for it when the farmers found their cows wandering all over the place. Sobel knew he was in over his head as a military leader. Knew he didn't have the men's respect. And, worse, knew he wasn't Lt. Dick Winters.

Winters was that rare leader who could be tough as nails but who respected us deeply. The result? We respected him. About the only rap on Winters, guys would tell you, is that he didn't drink on Friday nights with the rest of the officers; some took that as a goody-two-shoes deal, a cold shoulder turned to his fellow officers. But he was everything that Sobel wanted to be but couldn't. Sobel's pride got in the way. And when that happened, the only tool in his chest seemed to be the hammer. Beat harder on 'em. *I will make you respect me!*

By late October, Sobel—and, to a lesser degree, 1st Sgt. William Evans—had become the elephant in every Quonset hut on the post. The noncommissioned officers, in particular, were grumbling about Sobel, not because they didn't like his style but because they honestly believed his lack of leadership would be a liability to the men in time of combat. The guy hid behind his rank. Beneath the uniform, he had little confidence in his abilities to lead but too much pride to admit it. Instead, when he felt threatened, he'd use the power of those bars instead of his brains or, God forbid, his heart.

In England, out of the blue, Sobel demanded that Winters inspect the latrines. Winters did so. But later that day, Sobel, saying he had moved up the latrine-duty deadline and Winters had missed the inspection, wrote him up. Winters quietly bristled; nobody, he said, had told him about the time change. Sobel insisted he'd phoned and sent a runner.

That was the you've-pushed-me-too-far-moment for Dick Winters. In writing, he requested a trial by court-martial. Sobel responded the next day with two options for Winters: denial of a forty-eight-hour pass or being court-martialed. He assumed Winters, fearing the harsher consequence, would gobble up the revocation of the pass. Sobel was a gambler who thought he had a hot hand and could trump Winters easily. Sobel was wrong. He'd underestimated the man's integrity. Winters, his pride finally pushed to the brink, chose a court-martial trial so he could defend himself.

All hell broke loose. Fired up by Sgt. Mike Ranney and Sgt. Terrence "Salty" Harris, the noncommissioned officers basically mutinied. The noncoms called a meeting at which each man agreed to write his own resignation. In essence, they said, *We're turning in our stripes. We refuse to serve under this man.*

Tense times followed. There was talk that the entire company could be busted for mutiny charges. In the days to come, Lt. Patrick Sweeney was on-site, reciting the Articles of War that covered mutiny and sedition. Discussions went on for several days, one night until midnight. We were sitting in our barracks when Don Moone, an officer's mess orderly, came in and whispered the news:

"Sobel's gone."

We were soon introduced to 1st Lt. Thomas B. Meehan, our new company commander. Sobel had been reassigned to a new parachute-jumping school at the nearby village of Chilton Foliat.

So what had happened? I believe, with all the best of intentions, Dick Winters quietly orchestrated the deal to force Sobel out. Not for his selfish gain, mind you; that wasn't Winters's style. He was among the most selfless men I've ever had the privilege of serving with. No, he did it for the good of the men. He did it to save their lives. Like many others, Dick thought Sobel would lead his men into a massacre and so probably got someone like Carwood Lipton, a brilliant and trustworthy guy, to do his bidding. Lipton may have gone to noncoms such as Ranney—eager as hell for a commission and perhaps ripe to prove his loyalty to those above—and Harris, whose Irish blood may have inspired a touch of rebellion, to force the issue. That way, the intended goal might be reached without Winters's fingerprints being on the deed.

Dick denied it then, he'll deny it now, and he'll deny it till the day he dies. That's fine. But I will go to my grave believing that out of compassion for his men, he believed he had no other choice. And it was the absolute right thing to do. Ranney and Harris were both busted for their parts; Harris left the company and, as a pathfinder who jumped before the rest of us on D-day to mark our drop zones, died that day. Ranney went to Normandy as a private, became a squad leader in Holland, and, though he'd temporarily been set back, couldn't wait for a commission to be an officer.

By New Year's 1944, we'd been together for nearly sixteen months—and overseas nearly four. We'd been racked by a leadership crisis. Eaten way too much bad English food. And trained in nearly daily drizzle. Coughing and sneezing were now as much a part of the barracks as snoring and farting; the place now not only smelled rotten, but sounded rotten. Our spirits were low.

One day, Tom Burgess, a fellow Northwesterner, came to me.

"So, Malark, d'ya see the order about submarine service?"

I had not, so went to check out the new notice pinned on the bulletin board. There was a critical need for enlisted men to transfer. Burgess, a clotheshorse, thought it would be nice to wear neatly pressed slacks instead of the fatigues we were always in. I just wanted a change of scenery, someplace else to play out whatever "adventure" was in me. But I wasn't interested in going if Skip was staying.

"Whataya think?" I said after explaining the idea to Skip. He was all for it, too, so the three of us went to company headquarters to fill out application forms.

"Get the hell out of here," some noncom told us.

We weren't going anywhere else, except into the sky in planes, then down on the ground to fight Germans. And sooner rather than later, which, at this point, seemed like a blessing.

If Meehan was a welcome change for Easy Company, his arrival didn't mean we weren't without leadership problems—perhaps not at the top, but at the sergeant level. In the late spring, when Winters asked me to be a squad leader, I said yes, not that I had any design on climbing the ranks, but for the same reason some people run for political office. Not because they're passionate about politics, but because they're tired of being jerked around by the nitwits who get elected. By guys like 1st Sgt. William Evans.

In April, I contracted a severe head cold in the rainy, cold English weather. I went on sick call several times, was given some aspirin, and returned to field duty. But when the cold persisted, I got frustrated. I took a weekend pass to London in search of help.

I had plenty of money from dice games so I talked Burgess, who was broke, into coming along. On the train ride to London, my ears started aching terribly, worse than any of the ear problems I'd had as a kid or as a freshman at the University of Oregon when I'd had to miss the ROTC test. When we arrived, I told the cabdriver, "Get me to the nearest army medical facility. Fast!"

A doctor—a woman, which was rare in those days—discovered I had a temperature of over 105 degrees. She looked Burgess's way. "Get that soldier out of here," she said.

"But he doesn't have any money," I said. I started reaching for my money belt.

"He'll need to come back tomorrow," she said, and all but

shoved him out. Apparently this was serious and the docs didn't want any intrusions.

I was given oral medicine and massive shots of penicillin. In the middle of the night, I awoke feeling a dampness on my face and pillow. Blood, I realized, was draining from my ears and nose. They gave me more shots.

At 9:00 A.M., they told me I was going to be moved to the U.S. Army 1st General Hospital in St. Albans, about twenty miles west of London. I explained that I had a friend who had come with me; he could get a message to my company about what had happened to me. But he didn't have any money. They agreed to wait. Tom arrived. I gave him my money belt with over a hundred pounds in it and told him to notify the Easy Company officers about my situation. He said he would. At St. Albans, a full colonel was put in charge of me.

"You're lucky you got to a hospital when you did, Private Malarkey," said the doctor. "A day longer and the infection would have gone into your brain. And that'd have meant big trouble. Your battalion docs didn't do you any favors by missing this."

I was there for two weeks. They were shooting 250,000 units of penicillin in me every two hours. I hardly had any place on my body they hadn't stuck that damn needle. Finally, the infection let up.

"Given your problem now and your history with ear problems, you've got no business jumping out of an airplane," the doctor said. "I can have you removed from the paratroopers. In fact, I *should* have you removed."

The words hit like a punch to the gut. "Doc, no, you can't do that."

"But you're endangering yourself, Private. And you might be endangering the men around you as well."

Suddenly, I didn't like the way events were headed. "I've come this far," I said, "and I'm not quitting now. I'm a paratrooper, Doc. And I wanna stay a paratrooper."

"Even if it might cause permanent damage?"

"Look, it's like I was meant to jump out of those planes with these guys. Like this is what I was born for. Please, Doc."

He looked at me. "I'm going to let you loose for a few days in St. Albans as a test to see how you hold up. You pass, you're out of here, with no recommendation from me to give up the jumping, but if you black out up there in the sky, don't come crying to me."

I passed the test. But my return to Easy Company wasn't as glorious.

"Hey, Malark, thought you were AWOL," said a soldier as I headed for company headquarters.

"Been in the hospital," I said. "Didn't Burgess notify Evans?"

I walked in. First Sgt. William Evans looked at me as if I'd just made a pass at his girl.

"Where the *hell* have you been, soldier?"

I handed him my discharge papers from the hospital. He threw them aside, not even glancing at them. His eyes bored into mine.

"You, Malarkey, have been AWOL!"

Evans drove me crazy; he was worse than Sobel, a guy who was *nothing* but thought he was *something*. Another of these noncoms who was in it just for the extra fifty bucks a month. A guy who might even have put Sobel up to some of the tricks he played on us. What he had against me, I'm not sure. But whatever it was, it was becoming mutual.

"I've been in the hospital," I said. "Private Burgess was with me and I instructed him to notify you about my situation." (He had, I would later learn, though Evans kept insisting that Burgess was lying to cover my butt.)

"I got half a mind to court-martial you, soldier. You—"

Just then the half-ajar door flung wide-open from the office of 1st Lt. Thomas Meehan, Sobel's replacement. "Sergeant Evans, in my office. Now!"

Evans returned, trying hard to downplay the sheepish look on his face. Meehan watched from behind. "Report to your quarters, Malarkey," said Evans, the wind clearly out of his sails.

Meehan returned to his office. But my Irish temper had been triggered—and I sensed a rare window of opportunity. I looked around and saw a box of condoms, available to soldiers on leave who wanted to avoid the clap. I grabbed one of the rubbers and tossed it at Evans.

"Here," I said. "Slip that over your head, Sarge. It should fit every part of your body." And walked out.

As summer neared, such touches of humor were fewer and farther between in Easy Company. We knew we were going to be invading France; when, where, was anybody's guess. Meanwhile, with England now sprinkled with soldiers who'd fought in North Africa, Sicily, or Italy—and sharing stories with those of us who hadn't—war suddenly started having context. It was no longer like looking through a drizzly English pub window. It was crystal-clear stories of American soldiers fighting, dying, being wounded, and being taken POW. Sometime, while we were in Aldbourne—not just before we headed for Normandy as in the HBO miniseries—Bill Guarnere got word that his brother had been killed in Italy.

On my last weekend pass, I went with Skip Muck, Joe Toye, and Chuck Grant for a drink with a guy named Fritz Niland. A paratrooper in the 101st Airborne Division's 501st Parachute Infantry Regiment, Niland was a good friend of Skip's because they'd both grown up near each other in upstate New York. Fritz's brother Bob, with the 505th Parachute Infantry Regiment of the 82nd Airborne, joined us at a large pub in London's industrial district.

Like any time guys got together, there was lots of laughing, such as when Fritz told about getting blown off course following a practice jump in England, and crashing through the thatched roof of a house, landing on the table of a couple just getting ready to eat. Not missing a beat, they stood up, introduced themselves, and asked if Fritz would like to join them for dinner.

But what seared deeper into my memory was Bob's stories about war. For what seemed like hours, he gripped us with tales of his combat experiences. His punch lines at the end of every description were haunting: "If you want to be a hero, the Germans will make one out of you—dead." In part because he repeated the phrase and in part because it reminded me that, after years of training, there truly *was* an enemy out there waiting for us, those words tumbled over in my mind for weeks to come.

When I hurt a leg on a practice jump in Salisbury Plain, a Red Cross worker brought me a book in the hospital. The title intrigued me: *Out of the Night* by Jan Valtin. Immediately, William Ernest Henley's poem—the one I'd memorized at the University of Oregon—came to mind *(Out of the night that covers me / Black as the Pit from pole to pole)*. The book described the capture, by the Gestapo, of a spy who had done undercover work in various parts of the world, including the United States. When he was returned to Germany, he was tortured for 101 days and nights, but did not reveal the information sought by the Gestapo. It was a chilling thought: captured by the Germans. I hadn't thought much about that.

We had talked about the possibility in our training sessions, how we would only give them name, rank, and serial number, and how, as paratroopers, we were likely to be tortured. But, until now, I hadn't thought that it could actually happen. Despite such fears, we were getting so antsy we just wanted to go.

"Let's jump," said Skip Muck one night as we lay in our bunks. "I'm so damn anxious to get this thing started."

We all were. In a letter to my uncle Hugh in Portland on April 18, 1944, I wrote, "[I'm] feeling like a million and am all set to carry the mail against the Germans when the invasion comes, if ever." I said as much in letters to Bernice, too. By now, my on-again, off-again relationship with Bernice was back on; as at Toccoa, I'd gotten lonely in England and realized what a stupid idiot I'd been, and for reasons beyond me, she'd taken me back.

In May, on our last practice jump before Normandy, I was told to "jump" the mortar complete—tube, base plate, and bipod—in a canvas bag. "If you're not killed," said Lieutenant Winters, "that's how we'll do it over Normandy." I wasn't and we did.

Finally, our practice jumps were all behind us, nearly three dozen total, including a handful at night. We moved to a place called Upottery, about twenty miles west of Southampton on the English Channel, just north of Lyme Bay, though we weren't supposed to know it at the time because we were in total-blackout conditions. Nobody was allowed in or out of our camp. You'd be out walking around and see our own guys dressed in German uniforms to familiarize ourselves with the enemy. We'd come to this place to make sure all the logistics to support the invasion were watertight and, at the same time, to throw off any enemy-agent surveillance of the 101st Airborne. We were placed in tents along the edge of protected fields; armed guards surrounded us at all times, making it all but impossible for someone to run off and, accidentally or on purpose, reveal our invasion plans.

It had been twenty-one months since I'd arrived at Toccoa. We'd discussed how to attack gun positions, bridges, and causeways. We'd gone over equipment, from gas masks to knives, from guns to Mae West life jackets should we, God forbid, land in water. We'd sharpened our bayonets. We knew how to dig a foxhole, take out enemy artillery. We knew the "flash-thunder" passwords to make sure, when we hit the ground in the night, that guys were ours and how, as a backup, to squeeze our metal dime-store "crickets" to identify ourselves as friend, not foe. We knew that if a German police dog was suddenly sniffing the barrel of our tommy gun, we were to shoot the dog pronto.

We'd examined and reexamined three-dimensional sand tables and maps showing exactly what the invasion of France was to look like. We were to fly over the English Channel and across the Cherbourg Peninsula. Specially trained teams of parachutists, pathfinders, would jump about an hour ahead of us. Their job was to set up special lights and radar sets to guide the rest of us in. Then, in early-morning darkness, we would drop about five miles inland from the Normandy beaches and make our way west toward Utah Beach. Our rally point was a little hamlet called Le Grand Chemin; we were to get there by 7:00 A.M.

We'd learned that the Germans had flooded the low-lying ground just inland from the beach, forcing troops from the Channel to use only four causeways. Our job was to seize these causeways and get control of those exits so the Germans' supplies couldn't get to their troops near the beach and so our boys on the beach could get inland quickly. That might mean destroying the big guns we knew the Germans would have hammering the beach.

We'd been issued ammo and $10 worth of French francs. We'd even taken out our $10,000 life insurance policies, laughing about it to each other but not to ourselves.

The anticipation built to a sweaty-palmed pitch, then, as the wind started whipping around, crashed with a single announcement from General Taylor. Eisenhower had scrubbed the jump for June 5 because of a bad-weather forecast. Cheers pierced the air; even if we'd been anxious to go, somehow the thought of a nice hot meal and a movie instead of jumping into the unknown had a certain appeal. The movie was Cary Grant and Laraine Day in *Mr. Lucky*. Later, as we slept, the winds calmed. The next night, word came down: The jump is on.

In the hangars, we got our packed chutes, which, I'll never forget, had this shiny stuff on them, something new called fluorescent tape so we could see them in the dark. In those hangars we were each handed Eisenhower's written message of encouragement. "Soldiers, Sailors and Airmen of the Allied Expeditionary Force! You are about to embark upon the Great Crusade, toward which we have striven these many months. The eyes of the world are upon you. . . . Good luck! And let us all beseech the blessing of Almighty God upon this great and noble undertaking."

Father Maloney, our chaplain, offered absolution to those of us who were Catholic. Skip had stuffed a rosary in his pocket that he'd keep with him until the end. It felt good to have a clean bill of health with God. Johnny Miller—he was from the South—was reading his Bible; he read that thing everywhere he went. Gen. Maxwell Taylor walked among the men, shaking hands and offering encouragement. There was talk of three days of hard fighting and coming home while the ground troops pressed on. Sounded good. Frankly, it sounded *too* good. But in the nervous quiet, I think a lot of us wanted to believe it could be true—even though I was thinking more like *a year.*

We synchronized our watches. Trucks brought our gear to the airfield. Some guys had blackened their faces with charcoal or paint; our 2nd Platoon wasn't among them. I grabbed my gear. I would be "jumping" all three parts of the mortar unit—base plate, tube, and bipod—all of it crammed in canvas bags and secured to me. Sixty-five pounds' worth. Made you feel like the tuba player in a band. On top of that, you had to get in a plane with it on, then parachute out. No sweat.

That and my regular gear, including entrenching tools, ammo, weapons, and food, meant I had nearly two hundred pounds on me as climbed into that C-47. It took four guys— two pushing and two pulling—just to get me in the plane. Years later, I met a guy back in Oregon who'd been there that evening, a ground soldier who was watching us get ready. He told me, "I watched all you guys loaded down with parachutes and stuff, willing to jump out of an airplane into the night and go fight, and I remember thinking, *Where else do you find men like this?*"

The guys in our stick took their seats, backs to the fuselage, nearly knocking knees with the ten guys on the other side: Buck Compton, Bill Guarnere, Salvatore Bellino, Joseph Lesniewski, Dewitt Lowery, Johnny Plesha, John Sheehy, Cleveland Petty, Frank Zastavniak, Edward Bernat, Earl Hale, Rod Bain, Bradford Freeman, J. B. Stokes, Joachim Melo, Thomas Burgess, Robert Leonard, Richard Davenport, and Joe Toye. Skip was on a different plane. The pilot was Donald LePard. We were "chalk," or plane, No. 70.

You couldn't help looking in each other's eyes. Each of us, I suppose, was thinking something different. We were a pretty serious bunch at that moment. Those weren't football helmets on our head this time, but army helmets, each stenciled with a white spade to identify us part of the 506th Regiment. But as I looked at each man, I figured if I had to go to war, I couldn't be going with a better bunch of guys.

If you want to be a hero, the Germans will quickly make you one—dead. Bob Niland's words paid me a few last visits, interrupted by Lt. Buck Compton going guy-to-guy to hand out pills.

"What the hell are these for?" I said.

"Airsickness."

"Don't need 'em."

"Take them, Malarkey."

"Buck, remember me? I'm from Astoria. I've bobbed like a cork over the Columbia Bar plenty of times and never gotten sick."

"Take the pills, Malark. That's an order."

I think that was the only direct order Buck gave me the entire war. So I took the pills, though, looking back, I think they were more for our nerves than our stomachs. As the engines cranked up, I was already drowsy. At the moment, I wasn't feeling anything profound, as if I was about to plunge into history or anything like that. All I was thinking was *Let's go. Let's do this thing we've been training for seemingly forever.*

It was about an hour before midnight. Because of the British "double-savings time," though, it was still light enough so you could see out. Not that it mattered. By the time the C-47 lifted off, I was fast asleep.

That's me, back row, third from the left, flanked by Skip Muck, of course, on my right and Denver "Bull" Randleman. Camp Mackall, spring 1943.

I'm on the right with my brother, John, in the middle and cousin Hugh Lacey on the left. Oregon coast, late '20s. I'm perhaps seven or eight.

My former girlfriend, Bernice Franetovich. University of Oregon yearbook photo, 1942.

Bill Guarnere, who would lose a leg at Bastogne, at Fort Bragg, July 1943.

Brecourt Manor and the battlefield where Easy
Company took out the four German 105s,
Normandy. I took the photo in 2001.

Carwood Lipton, me,
and Dick Winters at
Skip Muck's grave in
Luxembourg in 1991.
No tears.

My great friend, Buck Compton, shortly after his return from Europe, 1945.

Joe Toye on furlough in London, July 1944.

Dick Winters at Camp Mackall,
spring 1943.

Bill Dickerson of Tacoma,
Washington, top, wanted a
photo of Skip Muck and
me pretending we were
jumping out of a plane.
Bill was a good friend, but
didn't earn his wings.
Camp Toccoa, 1942.

First Sgt. Floyd Talbert and and me in Austria, 1945.

Burr Smith and me at Kaprun, Austria, summer 1945.

Jimmy Alley and me at
Camp Toccoa, 1942.

Joe Liebgott and me on leave, Atlanta, 1943.

Skip Muck and me at
Camp Toccoa, 1942.

On leave in Atlanta, 1943.

That's me on a practice, jump, Camp Mackall, spring 1943.

In Mourmelon, France, after Holland and before Bastogne, November 1944.

7
JUMPING INTO THE DARKNESS

June 5–6, 1944
Normandy region of France

For what Easy Company would later remember as such an eventful time in our lives, it was an uneventful flight. At first. We spent a couple of hours in the air, and somewhere over the English Channel, I awoke. In the distance, you could see the wakes of hundreds of ships as our fleet headed toward Normandy. The boys on those ships would get their baptisms to war come sunup; ours would come a tad sooner. When we were over Guernsey Island, we first noticed some light enemy fire. Nothing serious.

Compton stood in the doorway and looked at me. He winked and said loudly over the rattle of the engines, "We're gonna throw a scare into those krauts tonight, Malark."

We headed east across France's Cherbourg Peninsula and

straight for Ste.-Mère-Église. That's when all hell broke loose. Big guns thumped below. Searchlights rolled around the clouds, searching for the likes of us. Tracer bullets from antiaircraft and machine guns zinged through what was now darkness. Fires burned on the ground from planes that had already been shot down. For a split second, I was back watching those giant Douglas firs bursting into flames and heading toward our cabin on the Nehalem.

Our plane—one of eighty-one that had taken off in England—was dropping, dropping, dropping some more. Ack-ack fire from the ground intensified. The plan was to fly in at fifteen hundred feet and go to six hundred when we were above the drop zone. But we were already below three hundred feet. And sitting ducks for the Germans.

We didn't know it at the time, but our pathfinders—guys who were supposed to jump earlier from a different plane and give us a signal to show us our drop zone—had gone down in the English Channel because of engine failure. We also didn't know that, though the plane was to slow to about 100 mph for the jump, we were screaming along at more like 200.

We stood and hooked up our chutes to the static line. Guts tightened. I don't recall there even being a sound-off; everything was happening so quick. I was second or third in the stick. All I was thinking was *Get the hell out of this plane, Malarkey.* The ground, at this point, was our friend. The quicker we could get down, the better off we were.

I was anxious, not fearful. With the noise of the engines, the darkness, and the flashes of light giving an eerie look to the clouds, too much was going on for you to concentrate on any fear that might have lodged in your gut. The light turned green and stayed green.

"Go! Go! Go!" yelled the jumpmaster, screaming just to be heard above the din of the engines, the guns, and the wind outside. Compton jumped first. Then Toye. I was next, a thousand do-this-and-do-that thoughts interrupted by a fleeting thought of "Invictus":

Out of the night that covers me,
Black as the Pit from pole to pole,
I thank whatever gods may be
For my unconquerable soul.

Only later would I realize the amazing scope of the 101st's contribution on this night: Nearly seven thousand soldiers were falling into the darkness. It had been suggested, long ago, that we shout the name of Maj. Gen. Bill Lee, commander of the 101st, when we jumped. I didn't. "Currahee!" I yelled instead. And jumped into the Normandy night. *One thousand one . . . one thousand two.* I felt the jolt of the prop wash. The chute burst open. With a splash of moonlight on the ground, I could see a triangular piece of property to my left, between roads. I'd been floating for nearly thirty seconds. I caught a glimpse of what looked like a farm road. Not much else. Certainly not the elm tree I suddenly felt myself crashing into.

Some paratroopers, I'd later learn, would die in such trees, target practice for the Germans come daybreak. Some didn't even make it that far. In either shot-down planes or hanging limp from parachutes, with bullets in them, they were dead on arrival. But somehow I swung down on my risers, almost as if I were in a giant sling, like at Camp Mackall, and felt my feet touch the ground.

Bomba the Jungle Boy in a Strange Land.

———

I found my squad leader, Sergeant Guarnere, the guy whose brother had just been killed in Italy, in a field. I also found one of our assistant rifle-squad leaders, Joe Toye. But, initially, nobody else. Toye had jumped a leg bag, and when his chute opened, the rope that secured the bag released too soon. It was wound around his arm and forearm, then cinched down to his wrist, peeling off a thin layer of skin almost down to his hand.

"Joe, we gotta get that patched up," I said.

"Hell, Malark, I'm fine," he said. That was Joe Toye for you.

Paratroopers, before anything else, are riflemen. So, with our semiautomatic M1 Garands in hand, we moved toward what we thought was the coast. With so few guys to help, I chose to take only the mortar tube and leave the base plate and bipod.

Later, we'd learn that we'd been dropped several miles west of our drop zone, which might have been a blessing in disguise because our target area, we later found, was crawling with krauts. We had landed about three-quarters of a mile east of Ste.-Mère-Église, about five miles inland from Utah Beach.

We walked across the farm road I'd seen from the air and looked through a hedgerow. I could see a group of people standing in an orchard, about a hundred feet away. I pulled out my cricket to start clicking. Blasted thing wouldn't work. We were fairly certain they were our guys, so finally I just yelled at them and they responded that they were American paratroopers. Guys from the 101st, though 502nd Regiment, not 506th. We joined them; they had an officer who had taken charge.

We started down a road toward the beach, looking for a road that paralleled the coast line so we could get to Causeways One and Two. Suddenly, we heard the sound of hooves and a cart behind us. We dove into the hedgerow. Out of the darkness came three horse-drawn carts and a handful of German soldiers, apparently hauling ammo toward the beach. We jumped them, rifles aimed at their faces. The horses got jumpy. Our guys were shouting; their guys were shouting. We took fifteen German prisoners. We marched them into a group, rifles at their backs.

One of our guys spoke German fairly well, and we informed them that if we got fired upon, they were to remain standing in the road while the rest of us took cover. We hadn't gone more than a quarter mile when exactly that happened. A German machine gun started firing. We hit the ditches. The German soldiers all stood in the road, as told. Except for one. He dove in the ditch. Guarnere promptly shot him in the back. We threw him on the cart and he died later than morning. From then on, we had no problem with prisoners standing up as we took cover.

An hour before our boys in the air started the bombardment of the coastline, we reached the road that paralleled the beach, about a mile inland. We knew we weren't supposed to penetrate beyond that point until after the naval and air force bombing had ceased so we held up. Fields. Orchards. Farms. The smell of wet grass and gunpowder. That's what I remember as it started to get light.

We could hear big guns shelling the beach from the sea, bombs bursting after having been dropped. We knew our guys were coming ashore. Occasionally, you'd hear the pop of a rifle, the chatter of a machine gun. We ran into a bunch more paratroopers who were halfway assembled and told them that a portion of the 2nd Battalion was about a half mile east of us. Guarnere, Toye, and I left the group and headed up a road where our battalion and part of our company was supposed to be. We hadn't gone more than a couple hundred yards when I saw it for the first time: death. A sickening sight. The dead bodies of a bunch of American paratroopers scattered about, along with even more Germans dead on the road. It was strange because it looked as if both had been herded up and shot execution-style. The krauts had already been looted; I wanted a Luger, if for no other reason than to prove I'd gotten some revenge from the country that had killed my two uncles. But even if someone else hadn't beat me to the punch, I don't know if I'd have gone looking. I was too sickened by the scene.

We walked on, eventually reaching our battalion, then headed up the road. A bunch of German prisoners, about twenty of them, were clumped to my right, just off the road. All standing up quite tall, as if out of respect.

"Where the hell are you guys from, Brooklyn?" asked some wise guy in our company.

"No, Portland, Oregon," said a German master sergeant, just off my shoulder. *What?* I couldn't believe it—that the guy not only spoke perfect English, but said he was from Portland (not Eugene, as the HBO miniseries *Band of Brothers* showed him saying, for reasons beyond me).

"No kidding, Portland?" I said eagerly. "I'm from Astoria."

The company walked on. I hung back, amazed at this coincidence.

"I worked in Portland until 1938," he said, "and came home when Hitler called all loyal Germans to return to the fatherland."

"So where'd you work in Portland?" I asked.

"Schmitz Steel Company."

"You gotta be kidding," I said. "The owners of that company were friends of my family. And I worked for Monarch Forge and Machine Works right across the street."

By now, a few of my fellow soldiers passing by were giving me the eye.

"Well now, what do you think about that decision now to return to your homeland?" I asked, scanning his POW pals around him.

"I think I made a big mistake," he said.

"Malark, let's go," yelled Guarnere, peeved that I was fraternizing with the enemy.

I nodded at the soldier. "You take care," I said, and walked on. I'd only been at war a few hours, and already I was learning stuff I hadn't been taught in training. Namely, that the guy trying to kill you—and that you're trying to kill—could be somebody who once worked in an American defense plant, across the street from where you later worked.

Strange thing, war.

Our column—about 160 men—moved on to a place called Le Grand Chemin. E Company was still scattered from here to hell's half acre after the drop. Among the missing was our commanding officer, Thomas Meehan, whose plane, we later learned, had gone down. We had pulled together only twelve men, with two officers, two light machine guns, one bazooka, and my 60 mm mortar. The good news? One of those twelve men was Lieutenant Dick Winters, a guy we'd follow anywhere. We hadn't been there long when we had that very chance.

Enemy machine-gun fire broke out up front. Word got

back to Winters through a D Company soldier, Lt. John Kelly, that a battery of 105 mm guns was hammering hell on our boys on Utah Beach, just beyond Causeways One and Two. He huddled with other officers, then came back to us. Col. Bob Strayer wanted E Company, or what we'd gathered of it, to attack the position. Some were skeptical; this Kelly was a boxer whose face was all beat up. Some wondered if he'd taken one too many blows, not the kind of guy you want telling you to go on a do-or-die mission to capture guns that were sure to be well protected by soldiers who'd been preparing for months.

The well-camouflaged German guns—four of them, it turned out—were about two hundred yards up ahead, positioned opposite a large French farmhouse that, we'd later learn, was known as Brecourt Manor, about five miles inland. The cannons were hammering our guys on Utah Beach. We get those guns, maybe the tide changes; if we don't, who knows what happens?

The farm wasn't a nice rectangular block; instead, it had half a dozen angles to it, flanked by hedgerows, thick earthen walls clustered with trees and grass. The angles were to our advantage because they gave us more options and the Germans more concerns. The German advantage? A well-thought-out trench system where we had no idea how many soldiers might be waiting, rifles ready. Later, we would learn a truth that I'm glad we didn't know at the time: Fifty to sixty men were protecting those guns. We were taking about a dozen guys, meaning the enemy had a five-to-one advantage.

But Winters was a thinker; he'd be given a situation and he could, in about the time it took the rest of us to do an equipment check, figure out a plan of attack. In this case, he explained that he would take half a dozen guys, and Buck Compton would take another half dozen, including me.

"Just weapons and ammo," he said. "Leave everything else here." Along with Compton and Guarnere, I was to crawl through the open field and get as close to the first gun in the battery as possible and throw grenades into the trench. Others would flank right and put fire on the enemy position. Winters would lead the charge straight down the hedge. Ranney and John Plesha, a guy from Seattle, were to mount a machine gun and cover the open area. Some A Company soldiers joined us, too.

As we closed in on the guns, staying hidden by hedgerows, the cannons boomed, each round taking out our boys on the beach. I felt my gut tighten. Finally, it was time: Our machine guns opened fire on the right. That drew the Germans' attention. The rest of us placed some withering fire into the position, with M1s, carbines, and tommy guns.

When the firing ceased, Lieutenant Winters told me to lead the way across the open field. I took a deep breath and, carbine in front of me, started snaking my way forward on knees and elbows, rifle poised, staying low in the foot-high Normandy grass.

"Wait, Malark, get back, get back here!" He suddenly noticed I was out of ammo and all I had in my hands were grenades. He probably saved my life, which wouldn't be the last time. Instead, he sent Compton while I got more ammo. Compton snaked through the grass and dropped into the trench; a Jerry was no more than ten feet from him. The Jerry began running away and Buck turned his machine gun on him but it jammed. Buck waved us across.

Guarnere and I took off. Behind us, to our left, our guys were giving covering fire. *Hail Mary, mother of God.* The adrenaline pumped through me. I jumped into the trench about the time Popeye Wynn took a shot in the butt. I could see two Germans down the trench, firing a machine gun. I pulled a grenade out and threw it, but meanwhile, someone— Compton, Winters, maybe both—had opened fire and the soldiers went down.

A German lobbed a grenade into the trench, where Toye was lying facedown. Winters yelled, "Joe, look out!" Toye flipped over and scrambled to run, his rifle taking the brunt of the exploding potato masher.

Then I eyed the first big gun, scrambled out of the trench, and headed toward it, spraying the area in front with automatic-weapons fire. I saw a German making a run for it. I slid under the gun, next to a dead soldier. I tucked up under the gun, firing and being fired on.

That's when I spotted a dead German soldier out in the open. I could see he had a case on his hip, which I figured was probably holding a nice German Luger. Briefly, the thought of my two uncles flashed in my mind. I needed a souvenir in their honor. Now seemed to be my chance. It made no sense, of course, running across a field in the middle of a battle, but, then, neither did dying in the Argonne Forest at nineteen or going off to war as a football hero and returning to live your life out in vets' hospitals.

I bolted for the dead German soldier. "Malarkey, you idiot!" I heard Winters yell from the trench. "Get back here."

I couldn't turn around now. I was already nearing the German lying in the field. I slid in next to him, confirmed he was dead, and reached for what I thought was a Luger. Instead, it was some gun-sighting device. *Damn!*

Across the main hedgerow, toward the farmhouse, German soldiers had four or five machine guns in place. Initially, they must have thought I was a medic—off-limits to shoot—because they didn't fire at me. At first. But my "medic" designation apparently expired because as I turned to get back to the cover of that 105 gun, those machine guns opened fire like a late-spring hailstorm back in Oregon, kicking up dirt all around my fast-moving feet. A German machine gun sounds terrifying. Ours went *put-put-put*. Theirs sounded like the tearing of a piece of paper. *Riiiiiiiiiiiiiiiiiip*.

Somehow I made it back and I dove under that same gun again, which was dug into the earth and gave me about a foot or two of in-ground protection. My helmet fell off. I lay there, faceup, as bullets sprinkled the ground around me. My heart pounded, my chest pumped. The fragments of the bullets were dropping on my face, burning me. Finally, I turned over to prevent that from happening.

Guarnere, my squad leader, got alongside the hedgerow that protected him from the Germans. He was about five feet from me. "Malark, we'll time their bursts," he said. So I started timing their bursts. "OK, next burst ends, get your ass over here." We waited.

"Now!" he yelled. I ran for cover. And wasn't hit.

"Way to go, ya stupid mick," said Guarnere.

I had no retort. He and Winters were right. It had been a stupid move that could have—should have—gotten me killed.

I relaxed for a split second. German weapons were far better than ours; a German machine gun could fire at a far faster rate than ours, but the high rate of fire made it tough to control the gun. That's what might have saved my life at Brecourt while trying to grab a Luger that wasn't even there.

Soon Winters was yelling at me again. Cleveland Petty had taken a bullet in the neck. Winters wanted me on the machine gun between the first and second German guns. I fired that gun for almost an hour, shooting at German positions on the farm road along Brecourt Manor. Then Winters had me move west to disrupt any German infiltration coming in behind us. It was a lonely job.

Once, I heard German voices from the opposite side of the hedgerow. I threw five or six grenades down the hedgerow as far I could. Later, I saw two Germans crossing the west end of the field and fired a couple of rounds that probably scared them, but didn't hit them. My only wounds were from nettles—a far better option than German bullets.

"Malark, pull back to the trench!" yelled Guarnere after a while.

As we left, I threw a fragmentation grenade down the barrel of the first gun to put it out of commission. We returned to the road we'd been on before the attack. I found the mortar tube I had left there—the base plate and bipod were back where I'd landed—and fired a dozen rounds in the direction of the Germans near the manor. When I finished firing the mortar, it was almost completely buried because of the force of its being fired. I was trying to unearth the tube when I looked up to see the oddest sight—a Frenchman, an older gentleman, using a shovel to help me dig it out. I nodded thanks to him. He nodded back.

After a few hours of fighting, we'd knocked out three guns but couldn't get the fourth. A stalemate was reached, though Lieutenant Speirs and three men from D Company knocked out the last gun. We withdrew, unable to get reinforcements or more ammunition to us so we could clean up some machine-gun nests. Those who tried to reach us had either been killed, wounded, or driven off. Of our men, four had been killed and two wounded. The Germans had lost fifteen men. We'd taken twelve prisoners, scattering the rest. But Winters had a plan to finish what we'd started.

Joe Toye noticed a barn and we sauntered over for a little shut-eye; we hadn't slept in nearly two days.

"Where the hell's your helmet, Malark?" said Toye.

"Left it back under that gun."

With that, I nodded off to sleep. But not for long.

"Malark, Toye!" It was Dick Winters. "Let's go. Hang tough!"

Winters had secured four Sherman tanks coming inland from Utah Beach. We went back to Brecourt Manor with them and had them fire everything they had to knock out the remaining machine-gun nests. The tanks broke through the hedgerow with Guarnere, Joe, and me running alongside them. There was no German opposition. The enemy was quickly overrun, some fleeing, most dead. More than a dozen horses had been killed. Smoke from small fires rose in the air. Finally, it was all quiet, save for a few moans and groans from the wounded.

I recovered my helmet, which was good because I had a photo of Bernice tucked inside it. We reached the causeway that had been secured. Set up defensive positions for the night. And finally got ourselves some sleep in some bombed-out village. It was about 8:00 P.M.

War, I was beginning to realize, was like a deadly athletic contest whose score you seldom knew even while you were playing the game. War was fought without context; you seldom realize how your piece fits into the larger puzzle. Only later would we learn that taking out those guns had probably saved scores of lives of soldiers coming ashore at Utah Beach. That as confusing as D-day had been for the airborne troops and as many foul-ups as we'd had—of the thirteen howitzers the 377th Parachute Field Artillery Battalion dropped that night, the Germans wound up with twelve—it was even more confusing for the enemy, because we'd dropped over such a wide, scattered area we were tough to pin down. Lots went wrong in our air operation that day. But one thing went right: Because we took care of business on the ground, our boys had an easier time getting inland, and the Germans couldn't get reinforcements near the coast.

For his efforts that day, Winters received the Distinguished Service Cross. Along with a handful of others, I won a Bronze Star with Oak Leaf Cluster, my Luger-fetching incident having conveniently been overlooked by Winters. As I told Dick years later, "We were luckier'n hell at Brecourt." His response? "Whataya mean, Malark? We were *effective.*" He also pointed out that he hadn't called me an "idiot" when I'd run after what I'd thought was a German Luger. "I called you a *stupid* idiot." (Decades later, Winters would say in his book, *Beyond Band of Brothers,* that he chose me, Compton, and Guarnere for one group because we were "soldiers who instinctively understood the intricacies of battle." That meant a lot to me.)

Decades later, I would be a guest of the de Vallavielle family, who owned Brecourt Manor, and learn how the Germans had appeared at their door in April, two months before the invasion, and told them they would need to leave. An artillery battery was being placed there. The Germans allowed the family to keep running their dairy operation, mainly because the Germans wanted the milk. On D-day morning, those guns started pounding the Normandy coast about 7:00 A.M., before we arrived. After the battle, one of the farmer's sons, twenty-four-year-old Michel, emerged from the outbuilding where the family had been staying. He saw the dead bodies. Dead horses. Shattered carts. Then an American paratrooper saw him. Mistaking him for a German, the soldier fired five shots at him. Looking closer, the soldier realized he'd mistaken a civilian for the enemy. *My God!* Michel was rushed to an aid station on Utah Beach. He would live, but spent eight months in an English hospital—and literally decades wondering what had happened that day at Brecourt Manor. Not until talking face-to-face with me—not the soldier who shot him, by the way—would he find out the full story. He did not hold a grudge for being shot. Instead, Michel de Vallavielle would one day establish and maintain the D-Day Museum at Utah Beach in honor of men like those in Easy Company who'd liberated his homeland.

8

BEAUTY AND THE BEAST

Carentan, France
June 7–July 12, 1944

Normandy, France, was beauty and the beast. The sprinkling of land unspoiled by war was the beauty. We, the soldiers, were the beasts. I'd see miles and miles of fields and orchards that, in places, reminded me of spots I'd seen in the Willamette Valley while hitchhiking from Astoria to Eugene back in Oregon. Then, suddenly, I'd see the remains of a horse splattered by artillery, the legs here, the head there. In some places, a breeze would bring the smell of grass and trees; in others, the rancid odor of death. Germans. Americans. Civilians. Animals. Whatever got in the way of war. One of the biggest problems we were having was taking care of our dead—getting them buried. Some of our Graves Registration guys resorted to getting drunk to do their jobs.

BEAUTY AND THE BEAST / 103

In the States, just as we were all coming of age and getting comfortable with school, girlfriends, jobs, along came a war. In France, just when we were all getting comfortable with war, along came reminders of home. Truth is that, lately, we hadn't been able to get comfortable with either.

Pvt. Alton More came to me a few days after D-day—we were waiting for orders—and suggested we go into Ste.-Mère-Église. More was a rugged John Wayne type, the son of a saloonkeeper in Casper, Wyoming. He had married his high school sweetheart, and their first child was born soon after we'd arrived in England.

"Malark, I hear there's a pile of musette bags full of chocolate bars just waiting for a couple a guys like you and me to save from melting."

Frankly, there wasn't much chance of chocolate melting; Normandy was unseasonably cold and wet, for summer. The mosquitoes were thicker'n anything I'd seen in Oregon, where they can be plenty bad. And I was uneasy when I heard the bags had belonged to our soldiers who'd been killed. But we were bored and headed into town, the first liberated French village. We found the rumored bags in a vacant lot and emptied them upside down, looking for candy bars, rations, money, whatever.

Suddenly, More dropped to his knees and, in a voice almost inaudible, said, "We gotta get the hell out of here, Malark." I looked over at him. He had broken down and was crying. Then I looked at the musette bag he'd just opened. Inside were a knitted pair of pink baby bootees. Not another word was said. We put the stuff back and left. Humbled. And, I think, a tad ashamed at the disrespect we'd shown to our fallen comrades.

Near Carentan, a town of about four thousand people, E Company was hunkered down, prepping for a final assault to capture it. Carentan lay astride the main road running to Cherbourg at the tip of the Cotentin Peninsula. The Germans wanted to keep the town; we needed it to bridge incoming troops from Omaha Beach and Utah Beach, north and south. We were camped on a roadway leading to the Douve River estuary when, about 2:00 A.M., a terrifying siren screamed in the sky. I buried my head in a roadside ditch, thinking whatever it was, it was headed straight for me. The sound faded in a few seconds. But it came back, and this time I stood and watched. It was a Stuka dive-bomber strafing Carentan. I never saw another one the rest of the war, and I'm convinced that, as a psychological weapon, it did the trick. I reminded myself, *Never relax, Malarkey.*

The next morning, we were sent to the west side of Carentan. Winters had made me mortar sergeant of the 2nd Platoon. Compton was the platoon leader. We reached an orchard. Buck sent me up a tree to see if I could give sighting instructions on a machine gun unleashing harassing fire through the attack zone.

Ah, yes, Bomba the Jungle Boy back in action. I headed up the apple tree—far easier than the firs and hemlocks of Astoria—and turned around to give a sighting to the gunner. Suddenly, as I looked down, my legs went wobbly. I grabbed the tree in a death grip, fearing I would fall. Slowly—and trying to hide my fear from the other guys—I slid down the limbs and trunk. Goodness, if I suddenly had a fear of heights, how was I going to handle our next jump?

On June 12, on the edge of Carentan, the 506th's 2nd Battalion, of which the 2nd Platoon was part, was walking down a road, readying for our all-important attack. It was dawn. F Company was on our left flank, D Company in reserve. Suddenly, all hell broke loose. One or two German troopers came out in the middle of the intersection, pouring machine-gun fire up and down the road. Mortar fire joined the barrage. So did tanks. They virtually stripped the hedgerow and we clung to the earth, cussing and praying in equal measure. The enemy fire split our platoon; the Germans were in a perfect position to wipe out not only our platoon, but the entire company. We scrambled to the ditches along the road, next to hedgerows, so panicked we were all but digging foxholes with our fingers. You had the feeling if you popped your head up, it'd soon be gone. It was almost as if the Germans were mowing down that entire hedgerow to get to us. It was the heaviest fire I would ever experience in war. Period.

"Move out!" Winters yelled.

Nobody moved, as if pinned in the ditches.

"I said, 'Move it!' Let's go!"

Still, nobody went.

Finally, Winters got hotter than I've ever seen him, and we got the idea: We reluctantly headed forward—early-game nerves, I suppose. When someone tossed a grenade to take care of the machine-gun nest, we had the intersection under control. The Germans withdrew. Knowing our positions, though, they rained mortar fire and machine-gun fire on us from afar. Guys around me were going down right and left. Winters took a hit in the lower leg.

It had been a fast and furious attack. At the end, amid moans of wounded soldiers and occasional shots, I heard the oddest thing: "Hail Mary, mother of Jesus, full of grace . . ." Over and over. Not the panicked voice of a wounded soldier, but the stoic, almost calm voice of someone else. "Hail Mary, mother of Jesus, full of grace . . ." I glanced up and there was Father John Maloney, holding a small cross in his hands and walking down the center of the road, administering last rites to our dying. Never seen anything like it, a priest administering last rites with bullets bouncing around his feet. Takes a hell of a lot of conviction, and faith, for a man to do that. Later, he'd be awarded the Distinguished Service Cross for his courage under fire.

Throughout the night, the Germans fired occasional shots. Were they going to mount a full-fledged counterattack at night? Needless to say, few of us slept well. What made it worse was Floyd Talbert getting gored by one of his own guys. He'd gently tapped another soldier to wake him, and the guy had, in a panic, turned and bayoneted Talbert. We weren't sure he'd make it, but he survived.

At dawn, we readied for what we hoped would be a final attack to drive the Germans from the outskirts of Carentan. Winters would later call it the "tightest spot" Easy Company found itself in during the war, though I thought plenty of others qualified.

We rained down everything we had on the Germans; they did the same to us. At some point, E Company was the only force holding the line; units on either side had fallen back under fire, leaving us out there like sitting ducks. We had a flooded area to our right flank, and nobody on our left.

"Malark, get over here!" It was Buck Compton, whom I'd one day count as one of my closest friends, but, for now, I wasn't sure I wanted to hear from.

"We need machine-gun ammo," he said. "You're elected."

My job, whether I chose to accept or not, was to scramble back to a farm building a few hundred yards away, across a pasture, near the intersection, where we'd deposited some ammo. I took off. Mortar fire rained down around me. I dove on my face and put my hands on my helmet. *Blam!* Shrapnel ripped into my right hand. The mortar fire stopped. I popped up and ran harder.

Go! Go! Go! I could see the building. Fifty yards. Twenty-five. Ten. I burst in the door, breathing hard. Our medic, Eugene Roe, was up to his elbows in blood, patching soldiers right and left. By now, he was already a seasoned veteran with the wounded, able to patch and diagnose in a quiet, methodical way.

"That's a Purple Heart wound, Malark," he calmly said, hardly looking up from wrapping a bandage around the chest of some soldier naked from the waist up. I looked around the room. The waiting line was long and full of soldiers far bloodier than me. I mentally gulped, never having seen the wounded congregated like this in one place.

"I don't want any Purple Hearts," I said. "But how about a bandage?"

He patched me up. I grabbed the ammo. And praying most of the way, I made it back to the hedgerows.

I refused a Purple Heart award because, in relation to what other guys were going through, it seemed like an incidental wound. As I later wrote to Bernice, "I refused it at the time for my wound was not bad enough that it was necessary that I be decorated. Death and mangled bodies are so prevalent I felt I didn't deserve it."

We had ten casualties in the June 12 attack on Carentan; nine the next day in the defense of Carentan. As that defense continued, we were giving up ground fast. The Germans were relentless. We were close to being overrun. Tired. Losing guys. And hope. But at midafternoon, the 2nd Armored Division—sixty tanks strong, plus fresh soldiers—arrived to relieve us. What a wonderful sight. Much better than when Sgt. Leo Boyle had earlier stood up and seen what he thought was a line of American tanks on the horizon. "Tanks! And they're ours!" he yelled. He was wrong. They were Germans. And he paid the price when, shortly after his pronouncement, a bullet riddled his leg. He was hit bad. And wound up being shipped back to England. It wasn't easy seeing your buddies go down around you. Beyond losing them, you wondered the inevitable: *Am I next?*

After the battle, Winters came across a German soldier who was terribly wounded and crying for help. He asked me to put the man out of his misery. I obeyed my order.

That night, over K rations in a gutted church, a story was told about Ronald Speirs, a first lieutenant in D Company, giving cigarettes to a bunch of German POWs a few days before and then mowing them down. That's nothing, someone said, Speirs had also gunned down one of his own men for disobeying him. Seems he had ordered one of his sergeants to attack directly across an open meadow at a cluster of farm buildings occupied by German machine gunners and a few tanks. Instead, the sergeant suggested he work up along a hedgerow instead of crossing in the open. Lieutenant Speirs took that as refusing a direct order, pulled his gun, and killed the man. There was no shortage of calvados and cognac in Normandy, and rumor had it that the sergeant had been drinking. In any case, the incident was reviewed by regimental commanders and Speirs was cleared of any misconduct. Still, I made a mental note: *Don't wind up with this guy as your platoon leader.*

The 506th moved to a defensive position southwest of Carentan. On the second day we were there, an American soldier was coming down the hedgerow asking for me or Skip Muck. I looked up from my foxhole. There stood Fritz Niland, the 501st Parachute Infantry Regiment guy whom we'd last seen at the pub in England when he was with his brother, Bob.

"How the hell are you, Fritz?"

He seemed distracted. "Seen Skip?" he asked.

"He's in the First Platoon, just about a hundred yards down the line," I said, remembering that the two were friends from back home in New York. Soon, Fritz came back and said good-bye to me, saying he was headed home, though he didn't say why.

Later, Skip told me, his usual impish smile gone and his face almost in a daze, "Yesterday Fritz learned his brother Bob, who's in the Eighty-second, had been killed on D-day."

Bob's platoon had been surrounded and he volunteered to man a machine gun for harassing fire while others broke through the encirclement. He used up several boxes of ammo and was cradling the gun to move to another spot when he was shot and killed with a single bullet. I remembered his prophetic words in London: "If you want to be a hero, the Germans will make one out of you—dead."

But the rest of the story was even more chilling. "So anyway," continued Skip, "Fritz hears this news and leaves the Eighty-second to tell another brother, Edward, a platoon leader in the Fourth Infantry Division, about Bob, only to find Edward has been killed."

"My God," I said.

"There's more, Malark. By this time, Father Francis Sampson is looking for Fritz. Why? To tell him that *another* brother, Preston, a flier in the China-Burma-India theater, had been killed this week, too."

"So, Fritz—"

"Is the only survivor of four Niland brothers serving their country. He's being sent home ASAP."

I instantly thought of Grandmother Malarkey, who'd lost two sons in one war and never gotten over it. "My God," I said. "That poor mother."

The Niland news numbed me. I had to get back from this war. Alive. If for nobody else, for Grandmother Malarkey, by then seventy years old and worried sick that she might lose a third boy to war.*

Dick Winters needed a volunteer to take out a high-noon patrol. Finding none, he came down the hedgerow to me.

"Malarkey, you're nominated," he said. "Report with Rod Bain, and six others, at battalion headquarters by eleven hundred."

His statement was punctuated by the *ka-boomb* of some incoming shells; we were well protected in foxholes, but the incoming and outgoing "mail" kept the ground shaking frequently.

When we arrived at headquarters, we found that the patrol

---

* This incident, after being told by me to Stephen Ambrose in a 1991 interview, became the basis for the movie *Saving Private Ryan.* Lieutenant Winters has confirmed as much in a letter.

was a command performance by Lewis Nixon, Winters's close pal and the resident lush. Nobody could quite figure out why those guys were such close friends; Nixon was a full-blown alcoholic and Winters didn't drink at all. Anyway, Nixon had picked out a complex of farm buildings, about a mile in front of our positions. He wanted us to penetrate to the outbuildings or as close as we could get.

Joe Toye wouldn't be on this team; he had been sent back to England because the medics were worried about gangrene setting in from the skin being ripped from his arm during the jump. Bain was an automatic pick because of his radio and skills with it. I also picked John Sheehy, Dick Davenport, Ed Joint, Allen Vest, and two others; eight altogether. Hedgerows would provide good concealment. We moved out and soon saw one that ran straight toward the objective. We followed it for a while.

"Sheehy," I whispered loudly from a crouched position about six yards behind him. "Stop at the next hedgerow and the two of us will check out the lay of the land." Staying low, moving carefully, I went to join him.

Snap. I'd stepped on a twig. In an instant, a German helmet popped up out of the hedgerow not ten feet from us, though the soldier inside was looking off to the side, not right at us. I pulled up my tommy gun, bumping Sheehy. The German soldier spun. It didn't matter. John got him in the head with a full blast. The kraut dropped with an eerie gurgle.

In the distance, I saw other Germans, responding to the gunfire. *We're in deep trouble,* I thought. "Let's get the hell out of here," I said. And we did. We all darted back the way we'd come. Bain had it worse than the rest, having to haul that sixty-pound radio. Winters, after we'd reported back, realized the Jerries were thicker than he thought. "No more day patrols," he said.

I was weary. After two weeks on the main line of resistance, those of us in Easy Company were a sorry sight for the eyes—and hard on the nose. Our hair was matted, faces unshaven, uniforms grimy and stinking from our sweat. We'd had little sleep, little quiet, little hot food. In a couple of days we moved north, up the Cherbourg Peninsula. It was primarily a time of rest, relaxation, and eating French beef, a delicacy that we enjoyed to the hilt. On at least one occasion we had an afternoon trip into Cherbourg, which had been liberated in bloody fighting.

In early July, we moved back to a location near Utah Beach for eventual departure back to England and whatever else this war had in store for Easy Company. This time, our resident scrounger, Alton More, was getting more tactful in his finds. He walked into camp one afternoon carrying two cardboard boxes, one of canned fruit cocktail and the other of pineapple. We feasted as he told us how he'd gotten it from the main supply depot. Others joined him on his runs in subsequent days and we ate like kings.

The day before we were to board an LST for our trip across the Channel, More outdid himself.

"Check it out, Malark," he said, showing me a U.S. army motorcycle and sidecar he'd wrangled from the main motor pool and hidden in the sand dunes near Utah Beach. He'd asked Compton about taking it back to England. "If you can get it on that ship, I don't care," said Buck, who was in charge because Winters had been sent back to England with a leg wound.

The next day, July 11, More moved the cycle up to the fore dune. We had worked out a hand signal for him to ride over the dune. I had tipped off the navy personnel that we had a last-minute vehicle coming aboard, without mentioning it was an American motorcycle and sidecar. When Easy Company had boarded, Compton and I were standing on the ramp. I signaled More. He came roaring over the dune and up the ramp like some sort of barnstorming cycle king.

We were the first off the LST at Southampton. More and I rode the cycle back to Aldbourne. On the way, I asked him what we would do for gas, and he said we'd stop at army depots. He opened his saddlebag and pulled out a stack of phony fuel tickets he'd concocted, but darned if they didn't work. We had no problems getting gas. And so with Alton driving and me in the sidecar, we zipped through the English countryside with smiles wide and fists pumping the air like a couple of carefree American boys who'd left the war behind.

9

UNCLAIMED LAUNDRY

Aldbourne, England
July 13–September 16, 1944

We were wrong, Alton and I. Though we tried like hell, we couldn't leave war behind, at least permanently. It came after us like a rogue wave, some three-story monster rolling toward shore, like the ones my old next-door neighbor, the bar pilot, used to tell me about. But soldiers, I was beginning to realize, got good at whistling in the dark. And so even though we knew that wave was coming, knew it was going to hunt us down, we sometimes threw caution to the wind and raced a motorcycle and sidecar around the English countryside all summer. We did this despite a message I'd gotten from Sobel informing me that he knew I had that motorcycle in my possession and would confiscate it when we left next for combat. In other words, he wasn't about to go toe-to-toe with Winters again, a thought that made racing that cycle around sweeter still, but would happily take on a runt like me.

We had spent thirty-five days in Normandy. Now we were back in Aldbourne and soon to be headed for Holland. What I remember most about this transition stint was more clashing between our lives as highly trained men in combat and our lives as ordinary guys in our early twenties who wanted to fish the Nehalem River or go back to a girl or return to play on a college football team but couldn't do any of that stuff so went to a pub instead. We'd tried so hard to outrun that wave, but there it was, building, building, building, and preparing to crash.

I'd only been back a few days when reminded of that. We had these two women in Aldbourne who did laundry for us for practically nothing. Great people. When I'd go to get our stuff, they'd sometimes say to me, in those beautiful British accents, "Cup of tea?" Once, one of them asked for a favor. "Might you take some back for some of the other men, save them a trip?" And started handing me stacks of clothes, some of which were for guys who wouldn't be needing those clothes because they were six feet under at Utah Beach: Miller, the kid who was always reading his Bible, died on D-day. So did Lieutenant Meehan, whose plane went down in flames, leaving Winters the commanding officer of Easy Company. Salty Harris, the noncom who'd had the guts to stand up to Sobel and then been busted for it, had been killed on D-day. So had Evans, the sarge who I'd had my share of run-ins with. Others who didn't come back were Sergio Moya, Robert Bloser, Everett Gray, Richard Owen, Herman Collins, George Elliott, and nearly a dozen more from Easy Company alone. Burgess, a guy from Washington State whom I'd met my first night in Toccoa, got shot through the back of the jaw. Some French farmer patched him up, held his hand, and he eventually went back to the States for recovery. But, you see, that's what so many people don't understand about war. When I told the laundry woman Burgess had been sent home to recover, she probably thought, "Oh, good," as if the guy had just fallen off his bike and skinned his knee. Actually, Burgess would need thirty-two surgeries and years to recover. And he was one of the lucky ones. On June 6, Easy Company had jumped with 139 officers and soldiers. When we were pulled off the line, we had 74.

You can't blame the laundry lady for not keeping a box score for Easy Company's dead, wounded, and missing-in-actions. And it's not like the British weren't paying for this war without some blood of their own. We all got furloughs when we returned to England, and a bunch of us checked into the Regent Palace Hotel in London and headed straight for the Palace Pub, owned by my friend Pat McGrath. Only he wasn't there. Soon after we'd left for Normandy, he'd gotten pneumonia. Had to go to the hospital. One night when the Germans were shelling the city, a buzz bomb—one of those V-2s—found its way into a heating vent, went to the basement, and blew up that hospital, taking Pat with it. So a woman hands you this laundry and you thank her and think, as you're walking away, *What do you do with laundry for guys who aren't ever going to need it?*

That's another thing they didn't teach us in the army. You train to kill and avoid being killed, but not what to do when someone you know *gets* killed. When we lined up, later that summer, for a memorial service for guys in the 506th who'd died in Normandy, it was new to us all. Back home, we'd seen our peers be honored at assemblies, graduation ceremonies, and the like, but, unlike now, never honored when they weren't around to soak it in.

We were bused to regimental headquarters on the estate of Lord Wills at Littlecote, outside Chilton Foliat, and lined up in fields of green, the entire 506th. Two thousand of us. A band played. A chaplain prayed.

Almighty God, we kneel to Thee and ask to be the instrument of Thy fury in smiting the evil forces that have visited death, misery, and debasement on the people of the earth. . . . Be with us, God, when we leap from our planes into the dark abyss and descend in parachutes into the midst of enemy fire. Give us iron will and stark courage as we spring from the harnesses of our parachutes to seize arms for battle. The legions of evil are many, Father; grace our arms to meet and defeat them in the name of freedom and dignity of man. . . . Let our enemies who have lived by the sword turn from their violence lest they perish by the sword. Help us to serve Thee gallantly and to be humble in victory.

General Taylor spoke but we couldn't hear a word he said; a formation of C-47s passed over about that time. But we heard the names of the dead. All 414. I never talked with any of my buddies about that day, but I wondered if we were all wondering the same two things: if the list would ever end. And if, down the road, our names would ever be on it.

While in England, I heard news from the States that Grandmother Malarkey wouldn't be worrying anymore about whether my name was going to be on that list. She had already lost two sons to war and didn't want to lose a grandson. But on D-day, said a letter, she had gone to church and prayed for the safety of the troops. Then had gone straight to bed—and never gotten up. My aunt Margarita later told me Grandmother Malarkey hadn't died of a heart attack, as the doctor had said. "She died of a broken heart, worrying about that curly-haired grandson of hers at war."

There were some crazy times down in England the last two months. Crazy good. Crazy bad.

I'd now been promoted to sergeant, and with it came a great perk: me and other noncoms, including Skip, had been given use of a private thatched-roof home on London Road, outside Aldbourne. Not that there weren't still rules, one of which was, no dames. But one time I came back to the house and damned if Bill Guarnere and Gordie Carson didn't have a couple of gals in leopard-skin tights holed up with them. And somehow, the higher-ups caught wind of it and were soon on their way over, in the form of 1st Lt. Thomas Peacock, a replacement officer and a big by-the-book guy.

Compton, who knew what was going on but wasn't about to do anything, called us from company headquarters. "Peacock's coming," he said.

Bill and Gordie were in a panic, but they found a ceiling entry to a tiny attic and shoved the girls up there. In walked Peacock, who said he'd heard a rumor that some ladies might be on the premises. Guarnere and Carson, like a couple of teenagers hiding half-empty beer bottles, shook their heads. *No, not here, sir.* Peacock, of course, wasn't giving up. Bill and Gordie stood firm. They thought they'd won this stalemate. Then it happened: A single spike of a high-heel shoe punctured the plaster ceiling. I'm not sure what

Carson's punishment was; Guarnere had to do close-order drills in front of imaginary troops. And, as an accomplice, for the first time in my life I got KP duty, along with all the other noncoms in that house.

Some of our fun was a bit more conventional, like me emerging as Easy's dart champion in the British pubs. Or like Glenn Miller's Army Air Force Band coming to put on a concert in Newbury. Miller's band was my favorite, and Skip's as well. Not only did I love his music, but I felt a kinship to the man. I'd been a Sigma Nu at the University of Oregon; he'd been a Sigma Nu at the University of Colorado. Each company was allotted six tickets. I went with Skip, Guarnere, Toye, and a few others. The place was packed, largely with well-oiled paratroopers and their English girlfriends, none of whom were particularly on their best behavior.

The first song was "Moonlight Serenade," which the band charged through beautifully despite a ton of gabbing from the audience. The band followed with the famous "In the Mood." Latecomers were straggling in and trying to find seats. After about sixteen bars, Miller's baton came down and stayed down. The band stopped on cue, as if somebody had pulled the plug on a jukebox machine.

I was stunned. Miller took the microphone and said if he heard one more sound from late-arriving paratroopers, the band would walk offstage. For good. Furthermore, he hadn't expected to see a bunch of officers hogging the front rows. Generals, colonels, and other officers went to work, turning into enforcers instead of listeners. It worked. Nary a sound was heard the rest of the evening. It was a highlight of my military life.

But soon after came a couple of lowlights. One night, me, Chuck Grant, Joe Toye, and a few others were in our room on the third floor at the Regent Palace, drinking, when Joe said he needed to take a leak and headed down the hallway. Fifteen minutes later, he wasn't back. With his good looks and boxer's biceps, we figured he might have run into some sweet British girl. But half an hour later, when he still wasn't back, we started getting concerned.

"I'm going looking for him," I said.

I walked into the lavatory. No Joe. I was turning to leave when I heard a noise outside. One of the windows was slightly open. Strange. I poked my head out. There was Joe, climbing out on the roof of an atrium. It was glass and fortified with chicken wire. It had to be strong, Joe weighed nearly two hundred pounds. It was three stories down off the sides.

"What the hell you doing out there, Joe?"

He froze.

"Please, come on back."

I wasn't sure if he was drunk, crazy, or a little of both.

"Joe, come on, everybody's worried about you."

For a moment, I wondered if he wasn't trying to do something drastic. Gradually, I coaxed him back and, when he was safely inside, looked him dead in the eye.

"Joe, what's going on?"

The look in his eye told me the question might have been a bit harsh. Because here's this guy with arms like pistons—toughest guy in the unit, period—and he's looking like he's about to cry. He started going on the way he did at the pub before we'd made our Normandy jump. About his childhood. His dad. Forced into the coal mines at fifteen. His not being able to speak or write as well as he thought he should.

"The hell of it is, Malark, I feel like a friggin' failure."

"You're no failure, Toye, and you know it. I've seen how

you gobbled up Currahee week after week. I saw how you fought on D-day with no skin on your left arm. And how the guys look up to you."

"I might have gotten a scholarship, played college football."

"And wound up right here, Joe, like Buck Compton and the other college football stars. Look, I'm not just blowing smoke when I say this, but you're the most admired man in Easy. Ask any of 'em. They'll tell you."

He brought his hand up to his face and wiped his eyes.

"Look, Joe, that you didn't go to high school—hell, that's not your fault. You didn't have any choice. We all have things in our past we regret—people we regret—but you can't unring a bell."

Whether it was the booze wearing off, my words, or his coming to terms with whatever he was wrestling with, he sort of nodded. "Let's get back to the room," he said. We never spoke of the incident again. And he always remained one of my closest friends, especially after my run-in with Dewitt Lowery.

In Aldbourne, I'd come back to the barracks after a night of pub-crawling and I heard some sniffling coming from the bunk across from mine. In the near dark, I realized it was Lowery, a kid from the South, sitting on the side of his bed. He smelled all boozed up, which, frankly, wasn't uncommon for a lot of us. But as I got closer, I realized he was crying. I put my hand on his shoulder.

"Dewitt, are you—?"

He bristled. "Stay away from me, Malarkey," he shot back, then flipped out his jump knife and stuck it right at my gut. I looked down. The point of the blade was about an inch from my stomach.

That's when it happened. These two strapping arms came

at Lowery from behind, lifted him up, spun him around, pinned him to the wall, and clamped a hand to his throat. It was Joe Toye. It scared the living hell out of Lowery. And, for a moment, me.

"Damn you, Lowery," he said. "You ever threaten Don Malarkey again and I'll kill you. Got that? I'll *kill* you."

In the morning, Lowery apologized to me. The irony was that what had gotten his dander up was the same thing that had sent Joe Toye into a tailspin that night at the Regent Palace: thinking he wasn't as smart as some of the rest of us. Lowery had apparently taken a lot of harassing that night in the pubs about being from the South, and not well educated, well spoken, or well read. And it festered inside until he exploded, in his case, with a knife to my gut.

That incident, Joe's incident, and one involving me reminded me that all guys really wanted—all *I* really wanted—was a little respect. And when it wasn't there, we all handled it in different ways, some worse than others. One evening, we were at the Red Cross Club when 1st Sgt. Carwood Lipton walked by. Lipton had suffered an arm injury in Normandy, and Don Moone and I let our Irish humor too far out on its leash. "Moonbeam" chided him as Lipton passed in one direction. I got him on the return trip.

"Hey, crip," I said. "How's it going?"

He grabbed each of us by the collar and lifted us from our chairs.

"You wanna get pulverized together or one at a time?"

We were too scared to speak. Lipton let go. "Hell, I'm sorry," he said, "but if this arm doesn't heal right, it could cost me my football career."

Everyone had a story deeper than what you could see—and some of us looked pretty damn foolish for not realizing that. Some stored hurts deep down, hurts that rose to the surface in some unplanned moment like that. Well, not everyone. I had my wounds. And I knew how to wound others with my selfishness; you could ask Bernice Franetovich about that. But, for now, I'd hidden mine real deep—in the same way the cutthroat trout on the Nehalem would tuck themselves back under a log or back behind an overhanging branch or in the shade. For protection, plain and simple.

Two months after we'd arrived back in England, Easy Company, loaded to the hilt in a C-47, left for a daylight jump into Holland and a whole new chapter of war. The plane, towing one of the hundreds of gliders that were used to drop men, artillery, and more, headed east, passing over London.

Though, after my dizzy spell in that Normandy tree, I'd worried a bit about flying again, it hadn't been a problem; once the rest of the 2nd Platoon had piled in, I wasn't about to stay behind. I kept looking out my window, not easy given that my back was to it and, piled with gear, wasn't exactly mobile. You could see P-47 and P-51 fighter planes on our flanks. We had escorts on this jump.

Training had been light since our arrival back in England. Combat jump after combat jump was planned, but scrapped, largely because General Patton's Third Army troops were moving so fast across France they were blasting right through our planned drop zones. There's no need for air troops when the boys on the ground are taking care of business. We cheered each report of their success; it postponed our return to battle. But nothing seemed to be getting in the way of our Holland drop, which involved none of the secrecy we'd used for the Normandy mission.

We headed over the Strait of Dover, and looking back, we could see the white cliffs. Soon we were over occupied Holland. We were homing in on our drop zone, about twenty miles beyond the front line of the British Second Army, just west of Son. We were to be attached to the British Second Army and be part of General Montgomery's plan to end the war quickly. Our objective was to take control of the north-south road that ran about forty miles from Eindhoven to Veghel to Nijmegen to Arnhem and its many bridges. To open a path for the British XXX Corps to drive through Arnhem and over the Lower Rhine River and into Germany. A massive British tank force was to breech the German lines and move straight to Arnhem on the path cleared by the Airborne. It was to be called Operation Market Garden.

I looked at the dozen and a half guys around me. Some new faces, like Babe Heffron. Lots of familiar faces. Leo Boyle was back in action after his leg wound in Normandy. My pan of the guys stopped on Eugene Jackson, a guy who, in some ways, had no business being here. He'd been seriously wounded in Normandy. Taken a large fragment from a mortar in the side of his head. Left a six-inch gash and took half his ear. But one day he showed up, reporting for full field duty, all wrapped up in bandages, looking like something from a Halloween haunted house.

A few of us went to Winters or Compton—can't remember which—and said there was no way Jackson was ready for duty again; the guy should be back in a hospital. Winters checked him out, agreed, and read the riot act to regimental medics who'd given the thumbs-up for his return. Jackson was returned to Oxford. But he'd recovered, and here he was, ready to go again. Ready to fight. I looked at him and just mentally shook my head in amazement. What an amazing bunch of guys.

Spirits were high. We were well rested, and no longer being hounded by the likes of Sobel and Evans, God rest his soul. Winters had replaced the unreasonableness of these two with a sense of compassion and fairness. It was clear and sunny over Holland, a rarity around here. High noon, September 17, 1944. Time to get this war over with, maybe by Christmas.

10

"BEYOND THIS PLACE OF WRATH AND TEARS"

Holland
September 17–November 26, 1944

As I neared the ground, the thousands of para-chutes near and far looked like so many jellyfish floating in the Warrenton boat basin back home. Compared to Normandy, landing in Holland was a breeze, the biggest concern being hit by falling equipment or a glider. No hedgerows. No flak. No darkness. We quickly assembled in a nearby wooded area, the Zonsche Forest. Suddenly, I heard a sickening sound in the sky: Two gliders had collided and, with a sort of pathetic quiet, fell to earth.

We moved east to the Son-Veghel highway, then headed south for our first objective: capturing the small town of Son and, more important, a bridge over the Wilhelmina Canal, just south. Capturing Son was a cakewalk—the Germans had fallen back—and now we needed to capture the bridge. But less than a kilometer from the bridge, our column was pounded by German 88 artillery and a machine gun, both coming at us from straight down the road.

Nobody got hit, but we were under serious attack. And that allowed the Germans to finish the job of wiring the bridge with explosives to blow it, a strategic move that would slow the Allied march considerably. Covering the east side of the road, Easy Company pushed forward, firing rifles and lobbing mortar shells, finally silencing the Germans. But not until they'd exploded the bridge. That night, we lashed a bunch of small boats together and crossed in the darkness. We would attack Eindhoven the next morning, E Company entering the city from the northeast.

As we approached the city of about one hundred thousand, civilians and partisans were eager to point out locations of holed-up Germans, having been under the Nazi thumb for more than than five years now. The Dutch, showering us with shouts of "Nice to see you" and gifts and invitations for food and drink, were far more helpful in this regard than the French. In fact, so many Easy Company guys had been sent to follow leads like this that Buck Compton and Bill Guarnere couldn't spare any more men.

But I was told to go with some other E Company men to check out one report of German soldiers holed up in a basement. I was packing a tommy gun. We yelled for them to come out, and lo and behold, they filed up like model prisoners—ten to fifteen of them. I was surprised at the ease with which they gave themselves up.

Meanwhile, others in Easy Company didn't have it so good. Lt. Bob Brewer was leading a patrol on the outskirts of town when a sniper caught him right in the throat with a bullet. He went down like a man who would never get up. The guys around him—I was elsewhere—saw the blood pouring from his neck, saw him writhing on the ground, and with no medic around gave him up for dead. But, when the skirmish was over, a Dutch farmer raced to Brewer, stopped the bleeding, and most likely saved his life. When medics came across Brewer, he was still very much alive. They claimed that without the farmer's help, Brewer would certainly have died. Instead, he was shipped out to England and went on to live a fruitful life, spending a good part of it in the CIA.

We met little resistance and had Eindhoven in our hands by late in the day, then awaited the Brits and the U.S.-made Sherman tanks they were driving. They soon arrived. At this rate, I figured, I'd be in Astoria for Christmas. At daylight the next morning, Dutch women moved through the fog, delivering cookies to our foxholes. What service! These Dutch were wonderful. But our walk in the park was about to turn bloody.

As we pulled a U-turn and swung back north, in pursuit of a tiny village called Nuenen, we moved through and were just on the outskirts when it happened. All was quiet. But, then, German machine-gun fire broke out from both flanks. A German panzer unit had formed a half-moon defense.

"Kraut tanks, kraut tanks!" soldiers were yelling. Apparently a panzer brigade, stationed just to the east in Helmond, had arrived with fifty tanks. We'd never seen an offensive like that. One of the tanks fired on a British tank and hit it dead-on. Flames burst into the sky. The panicked crew popped out, the gunner last. With no legs. The tank, on its own, kept moving forward, threatening to run over our own guys, who had to slither toward the enemy to avoid being squashed, the results of which we'd seen in Normandy. It wasn't pretty.

A second British tank emerged. It, too, got blasted. Two more went up in smoke. Two others turned and headed back to Nuenen. Easy Company fell back with them, bullets adding insult to injury on our retreat.

A handful of guys went down. One was Buck Compton, taking bullets in his butt. A handful of us made our way toward him.

"Get the hell out of here!" he said. "Leave me!"

We ignored his pleas. Eugene Roe, our medic, crouched to give him some help. Bullets flew around us.

"Let the friggin' Germans take care of me," Compton said above the sound of machine-gun fire and more. "Take care of yourselves."

Given the way we were being pounded, it seemed like a good idea, but no way were we leaving Buck. His size—he was 220 pounds—almost meant he'd get his way by default. But then someone thought fast: We ripped the door off a farm outbuilding and Guarnere, Toye, Babe Heffron, and I all but lashed him to it and dragged him to a roadside ditch until we could slide him on a tank, facedown since his wounds were on his backside.

I was always amazed at how black humor showed its face amid the horror of war. Carwood Lipton looked at Compton and laughed, having heard that the bullet had gone in one cheek and out the other. "You're the only guy I saw who got hit with one bullet and got four holes in him," he said. Compton didn't think it was as funny as Lipton and calmly threatened to kill him if he ever got off the friggin' tank.

Around us, guys were going down like bowling pins. Chuck Grant took a hit. Some guy—can't remember who— turned to jelly amid the hail of machine-gun bullets. Just curled up in a ball against some rock wall and tried to will himself back home or something. We'd lost four men; eleven others were wounded. One had gone nuts. So we did the only thing we could do: got the hell out of there—as in retreat. It felt rotten.

The Germans had Holland and weren't about to give it back. We wanted to continue heading north to Nijmegen on what we'd started calling Hell's Highway. Ultimate goal: Germany. Their goal was to get through to the highway and split our forces. They hadn't done it at Nuenen, but would try again. And succeed.

Near Veghel, we'd been called to an armored column of British tanks and vehicles en route north. For the first time in Holland, we were in trucks. We'd got reports from the Dutch underground that a panzer attack was headed northwest toward Uden, another town just north of Veghel. Suddenly, a German panzer task force slammed through our column, splitting Easy Company in two. One group, headed by Winters and including Skip and Toye, ended up in Uden. A small group of others, about eight of us, headed by Guarnere, were pinned down in Veghel, about three miles southwest. The Germans had circled the town with tanks and were shooting the living hell out of everything. Bullets zinging. Walls exploding. Guys screaming. The worst we saw in Holland. Pure hell.

Guarnere and I talked it over. We needed to locate the F company commander and explain our dilemma. Tell him we could, if he wanted, join up with his group. The officer told us to keep under cover; he'd let us know if we could be of use. We wound up in the cellar of a house packed with Dutch family members and neighbors on the north fringe of the battle lines. Outside, shells, bullets, mortars, and grenades had turned the quiet town into another stop on Hell's Highway. The noise and pounding wouldn't stop. We thought we were goners. Men and women were sobbing. Praying. Children were crying. The works. Not that we soldiers weren't about to pee our pants, too. For all we knew, the rest of our company had been blown from here to hell's half acre and before long the front door would get busted down and we'd all be learning our Heil Hitlers. Or worse. Later, we learned that the others in our company had assumed the same thing about us: that we were all goners.

The pounding went on for hours. Overnight. Wait and wonder. Minute by minute. Hour by hour. Would we ever get out of here alive? And what about the rest of Easy Company? Were they even still alive?

In the afternoon, things quieted down outside. Guarnere came to me. "Come with me, Malark, we're going to do some sightseeing."

We put on our helmets and went up the stairs. Slowly, Bill turned the handle of the door and swung it open. We crept outside, taking cover wherever we could. You didn't have to be Einstein to know we were surrounded. An occasional round of machine-gun fire tattered in the distance. A shell kaboomed a block away. A bullet pinged here and there. Safer, yes, but still not safe. Then I saw one of the most amazing things I'd ever seen in war: a British tank crew parked in the street, enjoying their four-o'clock tea.

Finally, some British planes—Beaufort tank busters— started diving on the German tanks on the perimeter of the town, and with help from British tanks and 506th infantry, the Germans were driven off. We survived, though we were fairly sure the rest of the company hadn't fared as well. Later, after we'd left the cellar and holed up in an orchard, we'd learn Winters and his guys had dodged death's bullet, too.

Behind enemy lines, Winters had stood in the belfry of a church in Uden, observing the battle in Veghel several miles away, fairly sure we were either dead, wounded, or POWs. Both sections of Easy Company came out nearly physically unscathed, but emotionally taken to our limits. When we met up, both platoons thinking the worst had happened to each other, it was a rare moment of relief, a moment that reminded us to never take each other for granted. We'd cheated death on that day, but we wouldn't be so lucky in the future.

We hunkered down in a drizzle. It was cold. The guys who'd been with Winters at Uden dug shallow foxholes. Those of us who'd just had the daylights shelled out of us dug so deep that we hit water. We pulled our raincoats over our shoulders and tried to sleep.

For now, the Germans hadn't been able to hold Uden and Veghel. I thought about those British officers stopping for four-o'clock tea beside a tank, a skirmish being fought in the distance. But after those tank busters saved our butts, I wasn't about to bash the British for tea-drinking amid war. On that day, they saved my life.

Several days later, a German force cut the road again north of Veghel. E Company was intact, just north, in Uden and was sent out to attack the panzer unit from the east. We were working with British tanks and had reached a pine thicket several hundred yards off the Veghel-Uden highway. Suddenly, from west of the road like a shark half-hidden in the shallows, a Tiger tank emerged, with just its turret and 88 barrel showing.

We had five Sherman tanks, being run by the British, attached to our company. Someone ran for our British tank
commander and took him to a sandy knoll, where the
Tiger could clearly be seen through a small opening in the
trees. He radioed for one of our tanks to come up. It spun
its tracks so its 75 mm cannon could get a bead on the turret of the Tiger. That done, the commander suddenly did a
tactical about-face, saying he didn't want to fire from that
position.

"He'll get only one shot from here, and if he misses, the
Tiger will take him out," he said.

No, he had a better idea. He had the five tanks line up
about a hundred yards to the south, in a narrow strip of
pines. They'd move through the trees and open fire from
the edge of the trees before breaking into the sandy field.
We, the 2nd Platoon, would space ourselves between the
tanks for an assault across the field to the Veghel-Uden
highway.

It proved to be a terrible mistake. The Tiger had seen our
tanks in the thicket and picked off each of the five—*boom,*
boom, boom, boom, boom—like a state-fair shooting gallery.
When the first one was hit, a big chunk of hot metal hit me
in the side of the leg. It tore a leg pocket but didn't hurt me.
Meanwhile, the tanks were ablaze, and guys inside screaming. With help from others, I climbed the turret of one and
pulled out a couple of guys from the panicked British tank
crew, not easy since a couple of them were on fire. The commander's hands had been blown off. We threw blankets and
sand on them to douse the flames and left the men for the
medics. Their future didn't look good.

We headed out into the open, machine-gun bullets tatter-
ing the sand. One of our guys, a lieutenant, went nuts and

just buried his head in the sand. Froze up completely. Scared to death. Sgt. Bill Guarnere was screaming at him to get his act together.

"You're supposed to be leadin' the damn platoon!" he yelled. When it was over, Winters got that officer right out of there in a hurry. He was later seen at an aid station, shot through the hand, the wound suspected of being self-inflicted.

I found some cover and started launching mortars at a German machine-gun position. "You got it!" yelled Winters. "Great shot." In the distance, the Tiger, having made quick work of the Shermans, pulled out. We might have been mowed down like fish in a barrel, but its machine guns were useless because the crown in the road blocked his line to us. Sometimes in war, your life is spared by strange things—in this case, by a Dutch engineer who crowned a road for drainage.

Operation Market Garden seemed as if it was becoming a waste of time—and of men. We'd lost about two dozen since the jump into Holland. James Miller, Raymond Schmitz, and Robert Van Klinken had been killed; others, like Buck, wounded. We hadn't gotten the bridge at Son because the Germans had already blown it. Hadn't been able to get through at Nuenen on our way to Helmond. For the first time, we'd been forced to retreat.

It was raining, nothing new for Holland. The British food was rotten. It was harvest season. Lots of fruit and pears. But you didn't smell that fresh fruit as much as you smelled mud and rancid water; ditches were always full of water in Holland.

"Mail call!"

It'd been so long since I'd gotten a letter I'd almost forgotten what they were. Not that my one piece of mail was an emotional boost. It was an Oregon ballot. I'd be voting for the first time. Probably because an uncle whom I respected so much, Hugh Lacy, was violently opposed to Roosevelt, I voted for Thomas Dewey. I cast my ballot, sealed the envelope, and was standing around a campfire, with the others, when—*blam!*—a gun went off nearby. Sgt. Mike Ranney started cussing a blue streak. He'd shot himself in the leg, just below the knee, with the bullet lodged at his anklebone.

"There goes my damn battlefield commission," he said with clenched teeth.

Nobody coveted the prestige of a commission more than Ranney; he was an apple-shiner from the word go. And you couldn't help but wonder if he'd perhaps quietly been promised something from Winters for being one of the point men on the Sobel ouster. Though he'd never get that commission, he would recover. And never have to fight another day in his life. Not in Holland. Not in Bastogne. Not anywhere. All because of a bullet in the leg fired by a gun he'd pulled the trigger on, apparently accidentally. Looking back, I've sometimes speculated whether it was Ranney's injury—and his being shipped back home—that got me thinking about the same thing around that campfire near Bastogne.

We moved onto the "Island" on October 2, 1944, by truck. In the night. Our new mission was to fight the Germans on a three-mile-wide swath of land—farm fields below sea level, surrounded by dikes with narrow roads on top—between the Lower Rhine River on the north and the Waal River on the south. The Germans occupied the east half; we had the west. They wanted it all—now—and launched an offensive to make it theirs.

Easy Company was rotated to the intersection of the dike and the elevated north-south railroad between Driel and Arnhem. The position was a platoon assignment with a fifteen-hundred-yard gap on one flank and two thousand yards on the other. Two contact patrols worked their way each night to the adjoining units to compensate for the lack of troops. The Germans controlled the railroad dike, which required everyone to stay out of view of the railroad during daylight hours. Virtually all movement was done at night.

It was to be a five-day mission. Instead, we'd be stuck here until late November, the longest time Easy Company would be in the same place. The weather was cold and rainy. We started calling it Hell's Corner.

Dick Winters had been promoted to executive officer of the 2nd Battalion, meaning no more combat duty, replaced by 1st Lt. Fred "Moose" Heyliger. Winters liked him. I liked him. He was mortar guy, like me.

On October 5, Easy Company caught an attacking German unit in a field. It was one of those fish-in-a-barrel moments that was both exhilarating and sad. As the soldiers fled, they were picked off right and left, though some returned fire. David Webster got his "million-dollar" wound that day, and William Dukeman, a guy who'd been with us since Toccoa, died. Eleven Germans surrendered.

Later, a German "King" Tiger tank came into that area from Opheusden to the west of us. We had an antitank gun set up at the junction of a farm road, and as the tank neared, our gun opened fire. It was like a peashooter against a dinosaur; I doubt our gun did much more than give the German crew inside a headache. But after it was hit about twenty-five times, it started backing up. The left-side tread slid into a ditch and the tank couldn't move.

Shortly after the incident, I came across our crew that had done the firing. Had anyone gone up to the tank? I asked. Nope. I did and discovered the tank was empty. I believe it had some sort of escape hatch in the bottom. The next day I came back with a screwdriver and ripped off the manufacturer's plate, thinking it would be a good souvenir. I sent it home, just one of many items that my folks would leave behind when they moved from the cabin.

On October 23, I was called in by Heyliger for an unusual mission. Technically, it would be known as Operation Pegasus, though we all just called it "the rescue." A British paratrooper, Col. O. Dobey, also known as the Mad Colonel of Arnhem, had been wounded and captured by the Germans, but he escaped from a hospital, swam across the Lower Rhine, and somehow got in touch with Colonel Sink. Some 125 British troops, 10 Dutch resistance fighters, and 5 American pilots were hiding out with the Dutch underground beyond the Lower Rhine. Could E Company help?

Heyliger agreed to a daring rescue attempt. He picked his guys, mainly 3rd Platoon personnel and some others, seventeen total, ticking off the names as each of us waited to hear if his would be among them.

"Malarkey." You hear your name and it's a different feeling from being back at Star of the Sea choosing sides for dodgeball. It means putting your life on the line, in this case for a bunch of guys you didn't even know. But this wasn't Star of the Sea; this was the military. So, even though you were dog-tired and a little worried, you did what you were asked. *Currahee! We stand alone together.*

It would be like nothing we'd ever done before: cross the

Lower Rhine in darkness and bring back more than a hundred people who were behind enemy lines. It seemed simple on paper: two Easy Company riflemen per boat, my partner to be Herman "Hack" Hansen, a guy from Chicago whose nickname came from some baseball player he liked. He was a happy-go-lucky guy who'd do anything for his pals.

Dobey had somehow maintained phone communication with the underground; each night before the rescue attempt, the escapees would creep closer to the north bank of the Lower Rhine. So they'd know where to gather at the river's edge, each night at midnight, on our side, a British 40 mm Beaufort gun would fire tracer bullets. And on the actual night of the rescue, British artillery would fire incendiary shells into the high ground, west of Arnhem, to provide a background of fire that would silhouette those being rescued on the river's north banks, so we could see where they were. The British rubber rafts were to be hidden the night before the crossing in an inlet formed from high water surging into the orchards. Surrounded by trees like that, the boats couldn't be seen by German air surveillance or through field glasses from across the river.

At about 1:00 A.M. on the night we expected the signal to go, I was leaning up against one of the orchard trees, my back to Hansen on the other side. My gut was churning a little bit more than usual, and not because of the rotten food. Having practically grown up on the Nehalem River, I was comfortable on water—but, then, I'd never had to rescue people in the black of night, right out from beneath the enemy's nose.

That's the thing about war, you never knew what was going to be thrown your way: a drop from a plane, an attack on an artillery nest, a rescue across a river. The only common thread was the chance that, this time, you'd be among those not coming back. In war, chance follows you like the stench of your uniforms, wherever you go.

"This'll be a miracle if it works," I whispered to Hansen.

I'd hardly gotten the words out when we saw something flash in the distance, across the river. "Malark, it's the light," he said. "Time to go."

A red flashlight was blinking the V-for-Victory signal, our signal from the rescuers to come. Machine gunners from the 2nd Platoon positioned their guns, in case things went south and we needed support, though, at night, such an exchange meant a high chance of us getting riddled by friendly fire. No two ways about it: This was a high-risk, high-reward operation. We slid into the boats, nearly twenty men in about eight to ten craft, and, as quietly as possible, started to cross. We were the lead boat heading across the river, which was about fifty yards wide at this point.

One oar splashing a bit too loudly . . . one tommy gun clinking against another . . . hell, one sneeze . . . and, for all we knew, Germans outposts could open fire and send us all to the bottom of the river. About fifteen minutes passed. But about ten yards from the north shore, I lowered my eyes just below the bow and could see figures huddled on the bank, the fires from the incendiary bombs giving us just enough light to see silhouettes of them.

I eased myself off the bow, about waist deep, and held the boat. A group of soldiers, many British with red berets, were huddled together.

"You our passengers?" I whispered.

"Yes, yes, thank you, thank you so much," one whispered back. Others patted Hansen and me on the back. "Thank you, thank you."

We helped about a dozen get into our boat. Most of the escapees were British paratroopers, but in our boat we had two American pilots and a British tank sergeant commander from the 7th Armored Division, who were known as the Rats of Tobruk after their gutsy fighting in the sands of North Africa. Once we got to the south shore, we left the boats on the bank and took the escapees over the dike to a facility set up just for them. En route, the tank commander turned to me.

"Sergeant," he said, "thank you for rescuing us. Good to be alive, but I've had it. No more combat. This is the fifth time my wife has been a widow and that's going to be the end of it."

The entire operation had gone off without a hitch. As the stories unraveled, we were amazed to learn that the escapees had, with help, been infiltrated through Germany units, day and night, coming from a variety of directions. It had all been coordinated by Dutch women in concert with the underground. Some had moved down to the river's edge from as far as fifty miles away. And now all were safe.

Bill Guarnere, the kid from Philly, thought he knew how to ride a motorcycle. He was wrong. He busted up a leg after trying his luck on a German cycle and was sent back to - England to recover. Suddenly I found myself replacing him as acting platoon sergeant. We got hit hard in an artillery bombardment, E and F companies splintered with eighteen wounded, though none died. And we lost Lieutenant Heyliger, accidentally gunned down by one of our own guys on a dike one night. He didn't die, but, busted up pretty bad, he, too, was sent to England. His replacement was Norman Dike Jr., an East Coast blue blood with no combat experience who would later freeze like a Popsicle in the midst of an assault.

In Holland, I'd cross paths with Skip Muck two or three times a week, more if we were back in reserve. He was doing OK, though, like me, was getting tired of the weather. The rain continued; the most common smell was mud. Foxholes were like big buckets of water, and so when we found a barn or outbuilding or house, it was as if heaven-sent. The bad food continued, British rations. Mutton and stuff. Our beards grew and bodies stank. Shower? What was that?

Some people think of soldiers in war and imagine us fighting day after day, endlessly. But much of the time, it's like being an anesthesiologist: 90 percent boredom and 10 percent panic. Yes, your job was combat, but much time was spent getting from one place to another, finding out where the enemy was without him finding out where you were, maneuvering into position. And waiting. Always waiting. On the Island, we weren't in a lot of day-to-day combat. Mainly a lot of night patrol work. The 1st Platoon saw more combat than those of us in the 2nd.

At Driel, just west of Arnhem, some in E Company would listen on the radio to "Arnhem Annie," a German propaganda broadcaster. I'd have preferred a little Glenn Miller, but it was a hoot listening to her inviting us all to cross the river, surrender, and live in luxury until the war ended. We'd rather stink and eat bad food. Instead, the 506th's POW Interrogation Team, using a loudspeaker, invited the Germans to surrender to us. It became pretty clear that nobody was surrendering to anyone else, period.

One day, Winters prepped me for a reconnaissance mission, saying, "A British artillery corps wants to use us as forward observers from the south bank of the Rhine."

Knowing that the British usually used their trained observers for missions like this, I was my usual blunt self: "What the hell do I know about artillery observation, Captain?" I wasn't afraid of penetrating enemy lines, but was just not a specialist at it like some others.

"Funny, I asked them the same question," said Winters, "and they said all they wanted was vehicular movement detected between Arnhem and Wageningen. I'm choosing you."

Soon, I was huddled with Winters and British artillery officers, going over maps and aerial photographs.

"You'll need to build a camouflaged duck blind as an observation post," one said. "You need good visibility of the tree-lined east-west road. Report all vehicle movement and identify it in relation to predesignated landmarks. Report by radio to one of our officers who will be with Winters, south of the dike."

I nodded an assurance that looked more confident than it felt. But I'd have my ol' buddy from the Northwest, Rod Bain, along with his radio and rifleman Eugene Jackson. Good guys, both.

The operation would take place the following day, with my moving into the orchard an hour before daylight. The nightly outpost would remain in position until we relieved them. But about 4:30 A.M., as I was saying good-bye to Winters, in walk the guys on that outpost.

"What the hell are you doing here?" I said.

"We thought it was time to come in," said the corporal of the outfit.

I looked at him with disgust. "You thought wrong." Then I walked out. We hadn't even started and we already had a strike against us: nobody out in front with eyes on the krauts.

Why Winters didn't bust that corporal on the spot is beyond me. Sure, it might sound like a little thing, but in war, screwing up the little things could cost lives.

We moved into position. I selected an area in the ditch and, as instructed, took a machete and cut branches and reed grass to build the blind so I'd have visibility across the Rhine. Bain, who'd been lugging the radio on his back, and Jackson rested in a ditch as we waited for first light. In the quiet and cool of dawn, I whispered a quick prayer, then found myself leaning on William Ernest Henley, the poet I took to war, and his reassuring "Invictus":

> *Out of the night that covers me,*
> *Black as the Pit from pole to pole,*
> *I thank whatever gods may be*
> *For my unconquerable soul.*
> *In the fell clutch of circumstance*
> *I have not winced nor cried aloud.*
> *Under the bludgeonings of chance*
> *My head is bloody, but unbowed.*
> *Beyond this place of wrath and tears*
> *Looms but the Horror of the—*

What was that? Something on the skyline, about seventy yards up the ditch. I'd hardly got adjusted in the blind, facing east and waiting for first light, when I detected some movement. I kicked Jackson, who was behind me, and whispered to him about something moving in the ditch. He, in turn, alerted Bain. I switched the safety off my tommy gun and got behind an orchard tree on the edge of the ditch.

There was the movement again: a head bobbing up and down. I challenged him with our password. No response.

I fingered the trigger. But given what had happened to Heyliger the other night, I held back. Wrong choice on my part. A German police dog, a Doberman pinscher, was suddenly sniffing the barrel of my gun. *Shoot the dog pronto.* I remembered that lesson from somewhere back in training, but for some reason, I didn't.

I challenged the soldier again. Then, in the murky darkness, I heard a frightened shout: "Me friend!" Something was being waved. Something white.

"Jackson," I said. "Move up the ditch and be ready to fire. I'll use the tommy gun if there's trouble."

He scurried up the ditch, then turned his head. "Eight krauts, Malark." Eight krauts who wouldn't be here if our outpost hadn't left its position, leaving us wide-open. I popped up, saw them, and with my tommy gun kept them covered while Jackson searched for weapons. Suddenly, I saw him deck a soldier with the butt of his rifle.

"The hell you doing, Jackson?" I said.

"SOB was hiding a P38."

"Bain, get up here," I yelled, fearing trouble.

The German patrol was scared stiff, begging for mercy, thinking we were going to kill them. Thinking, apparently, that more troops were nearby and missing the truth—that we were more than a mile from the rest of our outfit. These guys could have taken us in about two seconds. Instead, they'd dropped their arms in a ditch and surrendered.

Bain scurried up to my side. I didn't like this situation. Eight prisoners and a full day of light ahead of us in open country. It spelled danger for us. Maybe we'd need to hold them until dark.

"Get Winters on the radio and find out what he wants us to do," I said.

Winters wanted them back for interrogation. Now. *Great.* We wanted to live to see another day, but an order is an order. We had about six hundred yards of flat grazing land to traverse, most of which would be in full view of German forces on the north side of the Rhine. We lined up the prisoners, facing the dike, with Bain on the right flank, Jackson on the left, and me following with the tommy gun.

I'd already made up my mind: If we got into serious trouble, I'd have to kill all eight. I had Jackson mount his bayonet to further convince them that we didn't want any funny stuff. I hardly knew any German but thought *mach schnell* meant "run fast." It worked. I shouted like hell and pointed to the dike. We scrammed out of the ditch running at a full gallop, dog included.

I thought Bain, lugging the radio, would have a heart attack. Then I remembered Currahee, how he used to charge up that mountain with ease. Still, any moment I expected machine-gun fire. Nope. We got them to the dike, well out of effective gun range. As we had them clamber up the side of a cobblestone dike, the Germans' hobnailed boots pounded on the stone. So much for keeping quiet. I ran to the front so our outposts would spot me, not that I had supreme confidence in our out-front folks after their bonehead move earlier that day. I just wanted them to know it wasn't all Germans. I'd already seen enough of our men confused with the enemy; I didn't want the three of us to join the ranks—and we didn't. We got the prisoners to Division without incident.

By now it was late October and we'd been in this soggy, and sometimes deadly, game of cat and mouse amid the dikes of

Holland for nearly six weeks. War wasn't like a salmon-seining job, where you knew when the whistle would go off to say "stop for now." War was more like musical chairs; you knew, ultimately, it had to end. You just didn't know when, where, and, at times, *if,* a possibility that seemed to be increasing as early November arrived.

We stayed in an old farmhouse surrounded by lots of elm trees. From time to time, we'd send patrols to outposts in the woods. One night, Winters wanted Bain, Jackson, and me to go into the woods for a good part of the night to see if we could detect any German movement on the railroad. We did so, keeping as quiet as three soldiers can be. Suddenly, mortar shells started hitting in the nearby elm trees. The radio squawked.

"What's going on?" said Winters.

"Mortars," I said.

"Get back here now, Malark. No fooling around."

After talking it over, we were almost sure the Germans had planted some sort of sophisticated listening device that had picked up the sound of us. There's no other way they could have known we were there.

Finally, the music stopped in Holland—and I still had a chair. The Dutch cheered us as we left Holland for France, yelling, "September seventeenth! September seventeenth!" to remind us of the day they'd been liberated. It felt good to be so appreciated, but we didn't feel like we'd won a damn thing. What was supposed to be a short mission turned into more than two months. We'd jumped that day in September with 154 men. A third were either dead or wounded. My friend Joe Toye, hit in Normandy, had been wounded for a second time.

About the only medals given to Easy Company guys in this

campaign were Purple Hearts, hard to understand given that we had been fighting for seventy days. In retrospect, it was the waste of a top division; I didn't have much respect for the British general Montgomery. He'd kept the 101st and 82nd in Holland far too long. When it was over, Dick Winters came to me and asked if I had anyone in the platoon to recommend for a medal. Seems the British felt they should be issuing some medals to the 101st. I believe he was fishing for me to nominate myself, and frankly I thought maybe I should.

"No, sir," I said. "Nobody."

11

THE KNOCK ON THE DOOR

Mourmelon, France; Bastogne, Belgium
November 26–December 18

When Easy Company, half-asleep in a convoy of trucks after a fourteen-hour ride, rumbled into Mourmelon-le-Grand, France, I was too damn tired to think about anything other than a shower and something soft to sleep on. Only later would I realize that I was in a place not far from where my uncle Gerald had died twenty-six years before. Château-Thierry was just next door.

Camp Mourmelon, outside the village of Mourmelon-le-Grand, near Reims, was full of history. Julius Caesar and his Roman legions had been here nearly two thousand years before. Beyond the camp, you could see remnants of World War I: the artillery craters and trenches and the churches, many featuring ornate memorials for those who had died in these fields.

Strange how history repeats. My uncles, Gerald and Bob, had fought in the "war to end all wars"; a lot of Easy Company guys' dads and uncles had done the same thing. A quarter century later, here we were, back at it. The wars don't end; the ones fighting them "end." I didn't want to wind up like my uncles. In fact, somewhere deep down, I think I was on a quiet crusade to show them I could make it, not to somehow shame them for *not* making it. No, it was almost as if they were with me in all this, and my making it would say, Look, we, the Malarkey boys, *we* made it.

Not that a sense of history hit home with most of the 506th. For most soldiers, in late November 1944, this place was just the next holdover camp before our next fight, probably a jump into Germany in the spring, we'd heard. Replacement soldiers were now sprinkled among us, wide-eyed kids either craving—or scared to death of facing—combat. They were only a couple of years younger than us but, in some ways, boys among men, given what we'd seen since June. We also got some of the wounded back, among them Joe Liebgott, Bill Guarnere, Thomas McCreary, and my pal Buck Compton, whose butt was on the mend.

"Hey, Malark, thanks for the barn-door ride back in Holland," he said.

"Now, aren't you glad we didn't leave you?" I said. "There's talk of New Year's Eve in Paris." Compton's eyes lit up. So did mine.

We turned in our uniforms, which, after the rain of Holland, hung on us like damp moss. Got paid, finally. Spiffed up the camp, removing all the propaganda that the Germans had slapped up while they were stationed here during their occupation of France. Did some light drills. And though I wasn't among them, practiced for the Champagne Bowl, a football game that was to be played Christmas Day. The food was light-years better than whatever that was in Holland.

On my way out of the mess hall one night, I stumbled on what looked like a good craps game, a good sign just after payday. I stopped and watched while a hot shooter piled up huge winnings. Hell, I thought, he can't continue to throw passes like that, so I started fading the shooter—covering his bets. So much for that idea; in a few minutes, I was flat broke, an uncommon condition for a guy who usually cleans up. *You idiot, Malarkey, how stupid of you to blow all your money without even shooting the dice!*

I stopped by to see Skip, by now a noncom like me, in the house we sergeants were staying in. A dice game was going on.

"Wanna go gamble?" I asked

"I'm tired of being broke all the time, Malark."

I felt bad for the guy. While I was sending money home to my mom, he'd been sending his money home for a nest egg for him and Faye Tanner after the war. After paying off some debts, he had only $60 left. I *knew* I could win us some loot with that. Never mind that I'd just lost $60 faster than Burr Smith could load an M1. Never mind that Skip had just mentioned that that was all the money he had. Remember, I was the guy who'd raced out into that open field in Normandy, dancing amid bullets, to get a Luger that I never even got. In other words, prone to risk everything on some cockeyed idea.

"Skip, loan me your dough and I'll triple it for us both," I said with typical Malarkey bluntness.

Muck looked at me and frowned, then shook his head and smiled that wonderful Skip Muck smile. He either had a loose screw or lots of faith in me, because he then stuffed three $20 bills in my hand and said, "There ya go, Mal. Go win us some big bucks."

With my trustworthy friend,
the 80 mm mortar, 1943.

On my trip back to Brecourt Manor with Mrs. Devallevia and sons, Michel, left, and Louis.

Irene and me on a
ferry boat in British
Columbia, 1948.

Irene and I
had nearly
sixty years
together
before her
death in
2006.

Our medic, Eugene Roe, in
Berchtesgaden, Germany,
spring 1945.

My graduation photo, Astoria
High, spring 1939.

Me in Zel am See, Austria, on June 6, 1945, a year to the day from our jump into Normandy.

Major Dick Winters, Austria, 1945.

Skip Muck, Joe Toye, and me at Camp Toccoa, 1942.

Sgt. Buck Taylor, left, and Lt. Dick Winters in Scotland, 1944.

The Sigma Nu House I lived in at the University of Oregon in the '40s. Decades later, it would be used for scenes from that crazy movie, *Animal House*.

Our Sigma Nu basketball team were "A" League champs, 1942. That's me, front row, center.

Skip Muck, at Camp Toccoa, 1942.

German Tiger tank in Holland, fall, 1944.

A trooper being "drummed out" out of the 506th. That's Sgt. Buck Taylor with the gun. Fort Benning, January 1943.

My uncle, Bob Malarkey, died at 31, six years after being gassed in France during World War I.

My great friend, Vance Day, with me at the HBO premiere of *Band of Brothers* at Utah Beach in France, 2001.

Woodrow Robbins, who had a professional gambling background, was in the game. Within fifteen minutes, Robbins and I had all the money from the other five or six players.

"Hey, Malark, let's go to the NCO club and try our luck," he said.

We did. I started out hot and stayed hot, gathering in dollars, pounds, and francs as if they were chinook, coho, and sockeye in those Columbia River seining nets. I got up to $3,000 in earnings, then $5,000. I was half-afraid to walk out of the club, thinking I'd get jumped. I returned to the barracks.

"Here's your sixty dollars, Skip," I said. "Thanks for the loan."

"Any time, Malark. How'd you do?"

"Well, put it this way: Here's your tip." I peeled off $500 for him.

His eyes bulged. "Are you kidding me? Hell, with this Faye and I can honeymoon in the Poconos for a *month!*"

I slapped him on the back and headed for my bunk to get some shut-eye. Things were looking up. Our stock of champagne from nearby Reims was up to twenty-five quarts. The war was going well. The German Luftwaffe had all but been destroyed, meaning no blackout conditions were in place. We were going to be spending Christmas in a camp with hot showers and food far better than what we'd just left. Maybe New Year's in Paris. Other than being home, what more could a guy ask for?

The knock on the door came in the middle of the night of December 18. That knock opened the door to the worst misery of my life. When you think about it, that knock has haunted me for more than six decades. A knock I wished to God would never have come.

I rolled over and looked at my watch: 2:00 A.M. What the hell was going on? The other sergeants in our barracks rubbed faces, stretched arms, tried to shake off hangovers. It was some yokel from division headquarters.

"Get ready to head out. A major German offensive is under way somewhere in Belgium. Caught us with our pants down. Already put a helluva dent in our line. So pile all your personal items in the middle of the living room and report to company supply to get whatever you can in terms of equipment."

Nobody said much of anything or started scurrying around.

"Now!"

"OK, OK," we mumbled.

Later that day, we formed into platoon and company formation to check ranks and weaponry. "Pants down" is right. Maj. Gen. Maxwell Taylor was back in the States, at a conference; he'd been replaced by Brig. Gen. Anthony C. "Tony" McAuliffe. We'd turned in all our gear for repairs after Holland, and little of it had been fixed. We were short on guns; hell, we'd been training replacements with broomsticks. We weren't prepared to go fight anywhere at this point, much less someplace cold.

We'd been given the same light uniforms we'd used in Holland. We hadn't been given a winter issue of clothes; our boots were neither lined nor waterproof. We'd all gotten wool army overcoats, but we had no long underwear or wool socks. We were an odd combination of vets and rookies; Easy Company's 2nd Platoon even had a replacement machine-gun crew that was Polish, though the guys' physical size at least inspired hope. While standing at ease, the gunner picked up the .30-caliber machine gun as if it were a cap gun.

We were starting to load into high-sided cattle trucks—a few hundred of them—when I remembered the money. I had well over $3,000 in my money belt that I wasn't exactly thrilled about taking into combat with me. I scrambled around and found Compton.

"Buck, can you take care of this? Get it put in a safe place?"

He found a division fiscal officer who said he could take the money as a soldier's deposit, but it could only be returned to me on discharge. I had no choice, stuffing a receipt for $3,600 in my pocket and thinking that someday, instead of washing dishes at the Liberty Grill or tossing salmon on the Columbia, I might finish at the University of Oregon and get a decent job.

Late in the afternoon, we loaded into a large convoy. It was cold. Soldiers were blowing on their hands. All sorts of rumors spun through the ranks: *The Germans had run over an entire American army and couldn't be stopped.* Worry hung in the air like the fog of our breath.

"Guess this means football practice is canceled today," muttered someone.

A truck with Skip Muck in back rolled by ours. I nodded and half-smiled. He did the same back. So much for hot showers, the Champagne Bowl, and New Year's in Paris.

More info spread. The Germans—the same guys we'd thought were too busy licking their wounds en route back to their homeland—had launched a counteroffensive. They'd blasted a hole in the western front, and American forces were retreating. We were headed for the Ardennes Forest in Belgium, where the Germans were rolling through with their eye on eventually taking Antwerp, the key Allied port in Belgium. Specifically, headed to someplace called Bastogne, which had seven roads leading to it and so was a prized possession for an advancing army. For now, we knew it only as another place we would fight. In time, it would be known as one of the stages for the largest engagement ever fought by the U.S. Army, the Battle of the Bulge. The Germans would have a three-to-one advantage in manpower and a two-to-one advantage in tanks. By the time it was over, twenty thousand U.S. soldiers—two towns the size of Astoria at the time—would be dead. But I would only seriously grieve the loss of one.

Packed into a cattle truck with no benches, I couldn't help but feel as if we were animals heading off for slaughter. Given what we'd find on arrival, that wasn't far off the mark. The trip took a day and a half, our convoy stretching for miles and miles. With the high sides, you couldn't see a thing other than the already weary looks on the other guys crammed in like sardines. With rutted roads, our stomachs were jostled from here to hell's half acre. Guys would puke in their helmets and we'd toss it over the side; it reminded me of deep-sea fishing off Astoria. I tried to stay sane by reciting to myself Kipling's "Gunga Din," a gritty poem that seemed to fit, written, as it was, from the viewpoint of a British soldier about a native water-bearer, the "lower order" who saves his life. En route to Bastogne, with little in the way of equipment, you couldn't help but feel like the lower order:

The uniform 'e wore
Was nothin' much before,
An' rather less than 'arf o' that be'ind,
For a twisty piece o' rag
An' a goatskin water-bag
Was all the field-equipment 'e could find.
When the sweatin' troop-train lay
In a sidin' through the day,
Where the 'eat would make your bloomin' eyebrows crawl,
We shouted "Harry By!"
Till our throats were bricky-dry,
Then we wopped 'im 'cause 'e couldn't serve us all.

It was "Din! Din! Din!
You 'eathen, where the mischief 'ave you been?
You put some juldee in it,
Or I'll marrow you this minute,
If you don't fill up my helmet, Gunga Din!"

With too many helmets filled, we snaked our way through the Ardennes Forest, on a high plateau, near the city of Bastogne. We were about eight miles west of the Belgium-Luxembourg border. It was raining lightly, the day so dank that the countryside, sprinkled with groves of fir trees, looked like some black-and-white photo. We bailed out of the trucks a couple miles west of Bastogne, the only part of the circle around the town the Germans hadn't quite closed. We moved into the village in a route march formation, hearing artillery fire far to the north and east. Unlike in Holland, nobody was outside waving orange flags and giving us cigars and free drinks and blowing us kisses. Except for soldiers, there was no life anywhere in Bastogne.

The 501st Parachute Infantry Regiment was preceding us so there was no need for scouts or other security. But as we marched along, oh, how I wanted a little of that Georgia heat we'd had while training.

"Malark, whataya got in terms of ammo?" Buck Compton asked. I did a quick inventory of my nearly empty pouches and pockets.

"One clip and a couple of grenades. No carbine ammo at all. In other words, squat."

He reached into his pocket and handed me a clip, then asked the same question of the guys behind me. It was like asking beggars for money.

The 501st had moved straight through the city, heading east, and immediately met German troops. They fought till dark. We of the 506th headed northeast on the Bastogne–Foy highway. That's where I saw the sorriest sight I've seen in my life: soldiers—American soldiers—walking the other way, alongside the road, against us. Heads down. Some bloodied. Boots covered with mud. Retreating.

"What the hell is this?" I said to nobody in particular. "Where they going?"

"It's not where they're going," said Toye. "It's what they're runnin' *from*."

We watched in near disbelief as hundreds and hundreds of beat-up soldiers passed us. Two of their three infantry regiments had been encircled and captured. Most of those retreating were quiet, not even looking up. A few mumbled this or that. One supposedly told Babe Heffron, "They'll kill you all." I'll never forget the look in their eyes: fear, a sort of winter version of the stories I'd heard of loggers trying to outrun the Tillamook Burn.

Like me, Heffron was a cocky Irishman. "Don't worry,

fellas," he said to the quitters. "We'll take care of 'em for ya."

Maybe so, though the retreat didn't exactly instill confidence in us. But what could you do? We started mooching anything we could off the bastards: ammo, food, the works. Hell, if they couldn't do the job, they could at least give us stuff so we could.

I saw a Sherman tank on the west side of the highway; probably out of fuel. On its far side, sure enough, I found an engineer's shovel. It seemed like a small thing at the time—a theft by a desperate soldier—but would save some lives in the weeks to come, which would absolve me from any lingering guilt.

We came over a rise in the road and could see the villages of Foy and Noville below in the distance. A massive wave of German armor was sweeping through Noville, about two miles northeast. We stood and watched. The scene caught us off guard and made our hearts beat just a little faster. Nobody said a word. We just stared. We'd never seen the enemy in such numbers before.

Once we reached Foy, we were ordered to high, wooded ground southeast of the town; in war, it's always an advantage to be above your enemy. In Normandy, we'd burrowed into hedgerows. In Holland, we'd used dikes for cover. Here, we were hunkering down in a forest thick with midsized pine and firs that gave way to a grazing field sloping down to Foy and, beyond that, Noville. Thick not only with trees, but bodies. Our guys and theirs. There had already been fighting in these woods. Intense fighting.

"Hell of an idea—that shovel," said Rod Bain, my pal from across the Columbia River, as we feverishly dug foxholes for Easy Company. "You'd think the army might have thought we could use those."

"Just pretend we're after long necks," I said, "really big ones, deep in the sand."

"God, Malark, what I'd give to taste a clam again."

The ground was wet and cold, though not yet frozen. Taking turns with just a few shovels, we started digging our foxholes, making what would become our homes for however long we were here. We outposted a man as our watch about fifty yards out in an open field, then, clothes and all, slid into our mummy bags, two guys to a foxhole, and tried to catch whatever sleep we could. It wasn't easy. Like the others, I hadn't slept for nearly two full days and was dead tired, but I couldn't help thinking about the mass of German soldiers I'd seen just down the hill, in Noville.

12

"WHAT'S A GUY GOTTA DO TO DIE?"

Bastogne
December 19, 1944–January 3, 1945

In some ways, my war ended in Bastogne. In some ways it began there. The first day was surprisingly quiet. Eerily quiet, the forest wrapped in fog, the trees like thick masts in Warrenton's harbor on some November morning. It was the kind of quiet you sensed would not last, even if it lulled you into thinking otherwise.

We heard bursts of machine-gun fire and an occasional whump of an 88 in the distance, but clearly the Germans were, at least for now, doing business with our buddies and not us. We couldn't see much. And the Germans apparently couldn't see much more, given that a kraut wandered within shouting distance and crouched to take a crap. We took him prisoner.

We were hunkered down in a dense forest that ran west to

east between Foy and Bizory called the Bois Jacques. We just came to call it Jack's Woods. The 506th was spread out along about a five-hundred-yard front, meaning, with 150 or so men, we were already stretched thin. Easy Company was on the left as we faced Foy.

To bide our time in the first few days, we'd expand our foxholes, which was getting harder to do as the temperatures dropped and the ground froze. But we chipped away, a little at a time. When we'd finish an L-shaped hole, it'd be about six feet in length by two feet wide, the long stretch for sleeping, the short for shooting. Three or four feet deep.

The resemblance to coffins wasn't lost on Easy Company, though the amount of joking dropped with the temperature. We were exhausted. And it was getting colder.

"Give me the forty-five degrees and rain of an Astoria winter any day," I muttered to Bain, my "roommate."

"Hell, Malark, compared to Ilwaco, Astoria has winter drought. We get more than eighty inches a year."

I blew on my hands for the umpteenth time. Nearby, Walter Gordon Jr., a quick-witted machine-gunner from Louisiana, was sitting next to his machine gun as if a mannequin, his head wrapped in a big towel with his helmet on top.

"Jeez, Smoky," I said, "why not just put a big arrow pointing to your head that says, 'Krauts, shoot here.'" He just looked at me, rolled his eyes, and shivered.

Bastogne was miserable and cold, but, for now, dry. No mud. Ice formed on mud puddles. And because of the cold and light casualties, none of the "death smell" of Normandy. An occasional whiff of coffee, cigarette smoke, and a navy-bean fart—that was Bastogne.

The snow started on the second day, December 20. Growing up, snow was rare in Astoria, though I'd sometimes run into it crossing over the Coast Range while heading to or from the Willamette Valley. In Bastogne, it fell softly at first, then with great gusto. Just like our exchanges with the Germans. A few small skirmishes occurred here and there, but not much else.

Father Maloney quietly gathered Easy's Catholics and others who felt the need for some spiritual encouragement. It was Skip's idea. Alex Penkala, another close friend of Skip's, was there; like Muck, he was a pretty serious Catholic. Perconte would make fun of him for still being a virgin. Me? I prayed a lot during the war that I could somehow just make it back to the banks of the Nehalem River with a blackberry tin in my hand. I was no Father Maloney. What a trouper he was, having jumped with us into Normandy and Holland, and being with us now in Bastogne. In the stillness of the woods, his words were soft assurance on the jagged edge of war: "God, the Father of mercies, through the death and resurrection of his Son, has reconciled the world to himself and sent the Holy Spirit among us for the forgiveness of sins; through the ministry of the Church may God give you pardon and peace, and I absolve you from your sins in the name of the Father, and of the Son, and of the Holy Ghost. Amen."

As the group broke up, Skip and I made our ways to each other, having not seen one another since Mourmelon. Our eyes—tired eyes—met. He was holding the rosary he carried with him everywhere.

"Stay safe, Skipper," I said.

"You, too, Malark. See you when we get outa this friggin' icebox."

We shook hands. He left to rejoin the 1st Platoon. I returned to my foxhole a few hundred yards away. By then, the

Jerries had moved machine gunners along the Foy–Bizory road. But all we could do was wait, knowing either they would attack or we would. Some will tell you that fear is a soldier's worst enemy. I disagree. Too much and you're paralyzed. But too little and you're dead. Fear helps you take care of yourself so something bad won't happen to you. If you don't have at least some fear, you're going to be a damn poor soldier and get yourself wounded or killed. Yeah, too much can kill you. But a little of it can save your life.

Sometimes, I worried as much about having rookies to the left and right of me as I did about the enemy. You'd always get a bit more nervous if you had some replacement beside you. And for whatever reason, they were the guys who seemed to get killed or wounded faster. Maybe it was because they just weren't as gritty. Or maybe because they weren't as well trained. In either case, they seemed to disappear quicker than the Toccoa guys.

Suddenly, on the second or third day, the stillness of the woods was shattered by the pop of guns and the sound of bullets ripping into trees. And then the awful sound of someone getting hit: a muffled cry. "I'm hit!" And the panicked cry of "Medic! Medic!" And a machine-gunning of swear words that spoke not only of pain but of the frustration of knowing the victim could no longer do battle with the bastard who'd shot him. And—God, I hated this one—a soft, desperate call for a mother.

The German machine gunners kept spraying the woods like a lawn sprinkler till we finally got some guys in position and started hammering back. Before long, the field beyond the woods was littered with dead Germans. Dozens of them, part of one small attempt to push the lines west, toward their ultimate goal of Antwerp. Not that every time we quelled such a push it didn't cost us something. Gordon took a shot in the neck that should have killed him but didn't. Same with another machine gunner. They survived, but not by much. Same with that new machine-gun crew, the Polish guys. Our medic, Eugene Roe, was busy that day, and the nearest aid station was in Bastogne, a few dangerous miles away.

Wounded men were Roe's stock-in-trade. And he'd seen more death than anyone else in the unit. To the rest of us, death was some rogue wave that would crash down on us from time to time. Hell, Roe was standing out in the surf every day, taking one shot after another. Since we'd got to Bastogne—bloodier than any other place we'd been—Roe was getting a bit of that thousand-yard stare himself. Quieter. You could tell it was getting to him. And who could blame him?

We continued hide-and-seek games with the krauts for the next few days, not that there was much daylight in which to fight. It didn't get light until around 8:00 A.M. and returned to dark around 4:00 P.M. We'd pick a fight, they'd pick a fight. They'd send a patrol; we'd send a patrol. We did a lot of frontline firing and mortaring. Perhaps too much. If this stalemate didn't break in our favor soon, we were bound to lose because we were already running out of ammo. And snow and heavy fog meant our flyboys weren't, at least for now, going to be saving our butts with a supply drop. We were down to six rounds per mortar, one bandolier per rifleman, and one box of machine-gun ammo per gun.

"No firing at anything, except to repel a major attack," said Compton.

Before long, the Germans seemed to sense this. When the fog would lift, we'd see them down there in Foy, frolicking around in their white snowsuits, almost as if daring us to come after them but knowing we couldn't. Already, the 506th's 1st Battalion had been beat up pretty badly trying to take the town and had fallen back.

Ammo wasn't the only thing we were low on. Roe was going from man to man like some sort of desperate trick-or-treater, scrounging whatever he could in the way of supplies. Food was becoming a problem. Not enough K rations had got distributed in the rush to leave Mourmelon. Our company cooks tried to get us hot, boiled chunks of beef in a souplike recipe—or white beans in broth—brought in from Bastogne by jeep before daylight or after dark, but it was impossible to keep it even lukewarm. Our best culinary trick was mixing a lemonade packet from our K rations to make an iced dessert. But, God, what I'd give for a hamburger steak and mashed potatoes from the Liberty Grill.

Meanwhile, the cold and snow started taking their toll. Joe Toye's soft singing of Irish ballads or "I'll Be Seeing You" might have eased his soul, but it wasn't doing much for his toes. Roe suggested he go back to regiment for a break. "I ain't comin' off the line," Toye said.

We were told to inspect our feet on occasion. Blue was a warning. Black the danger zone. On December 21, up to a foot of dry powder fell. And yet we were still wearing summer uniforms. All we had for cold weather were long, wool overcoats, which helped in the trenches but obviously weren't smart for combat, and thin woolen caps we wore under our helmets. Sometimes, if a guy got hit, Roe was having to tuck the plasma bottle in his armpit to keep the stuff from freezing.

"Krauts don't know how good they got it," said Bill Guarnere, who'd become a close friend. "Wearing them snowsuits and sleeping in houses down there in Foy—they got the life."

When you'd be up checking an outpost and look down on that village, you'd think you were looking at a Currier & Ives Christmas card. Then you'd stumble over some frozen corpse, bled out in the snow, and you'd think otherwise. The body of one dead German, not far from our foxholes, finally got to a few guys; despite the nearly frozen soil, they gave him a proper burial.

By now, I'd become a unit sergeant. Along with other non-coms, we needed to keep an eye on who needed a break, some Joe who needed a couple of days back at the command post, where Winters was, or being a runner between us.

"Malark, I need you to witness this for me," said Roe one day. One of our replacements —a guy named Hughes whose grandfather had been a U.S. Supreme Court justice— huddled in his foxhole, complaining of not being able to feel his feet. Roe unlaced one of the man's boots. His foot was half-black, early signs of gangrene. His war was over. Later, I heard he lost part of one foot and the entire other foot, though, as a newcomer to us at Mourmelon, he may never even have fired a shot in the war.

Once, I made the mistake of checking my own feet; took me two days to get them warm again. While picking up supplies in Bastogne, I picked up some burlap bags and started wrapping my boots in them. I found that if you poured some water on them and had it freeze, it actually worked as insulation and kept your feet warmer. I got a lot of heckling for my system, but by now I preferred warmth to pride and, while some believed otherwise, remained convinced this was the way to go. Speirs thought my getup was the funniest thing since Abbott and Costello; he had Forrest Guth, a guy with a camera, take a picture of me. Winters just thought I was nuts. Later, he said, "Can you imagine a guy wrapping his feet so he could *stay* in combat rather than get out?"

Every now and then you'd hear about some guy who'd taken off his boots just to freeze his feet so he could get out of here. Occasionally, some guy would go so far as to put a bullet in his foot for the same reason. War could twist your mind in lots of ways; when you get cold and exhausted, you lose your mental edge. And if you lose your mental edge, you lose hope. You lose hope and you're doomed. For some guys, a day or two helping out back at the command post could charge their batteries a bit. Winters was big on that. He'd notice a guy who was having a tough time and call him for a little break. "Hang tough," he was always telling us. Other times, the only way out for a soldier seemed to be the one thing I vowed I'd never do: quit.

Bastogne was challenging us in ways no other place had. We had no artillery power and no airpower. We were low on ammo and food. The men were cold, fearful, exhausted. I've heard a soldier loses his effectiveness in combat after about 90 days; we'd been in action for 107 since Normandy. This wasn't exactly how any of us had expected to spend Christmas 1944. As if our situation wasn't already ominous enough, word filtered through Easy's ranks from a medic back in Bastogne: The Germans had closed the circle. The 101st Airborne was now completely surrounded, but as Winters would remind us, "We're used to that. We're paratroopers."

Our Christmas miracle came early. On December 23, we awoke to clear skies.

"God, look at that," said Compton. "UCLA blue!"

"Listen," said Toye. "Planes. I hear planes."

We weren't dreaming. We looked above us; in the gaps between the trees and there against an almost-too-true-to-be-real blue sky were C-47 transport planes, dropping supplies: food, blankets, medicine, ammunition, the works. The amount would prove less than we'd expected—the K rations would last for only a few days—but they were *something*, and triggered a much needed boost in morale. After a week cut off from everybody else, hidden back in the woods, we'd lost any sense of context, that we were part of something bigger than just staying alive. The planes reconnected us somehow. Soon, a few P-47s were also in the sky, apparently to rouse the Germans below in Foy and Noville.

Some guys, including me, ran partway into the open field so they could see us. We whooped, hollered, and cheered, then suddenly froze in panic. *Ch-ch-ch-ch-ch-ch-ch-ch-ch-ch.* The P-47s were opening fire with mounted machine guns. On us.

"What the hell?" I said.

We scattered beneath trees and into foxholes, wondering if those had been our own guys accidentally firing at us or Germans who'd captured our planes. They returned for a second go. I dove behind a tree. *Ping.* A bullet glanced off my helmet, sending my metal cap flying, but leaving me unscathed. I'd had tons of close calls since Normandy; this was another. But, somehow, I'd yet to be seriously wounded. At Bastogne, though, you didn't find yourself thinking too much about long-range possibilities—say, getting back home. You were more concerned about just making it until tomorrow.

On December 24, a jeep from Bastogne brought copies of a one-page newspaper. The Germans had, two days earlier, demanded the surrender of the 101st. Beneath a "Merry Christmas" greeting, General A. C. McAuliffe had written:

24 December 1944

What's Merry about all this, you ask? We're fighting—it's cold. We aren't home. All true but what has the proud Eagle Division accomplished with its worthy comrades the 10th Armored Division, the 705th Tank Destroyer Battalion and all the rest? Just this: We have stopped cold everything that has been thrown at us from the North, East, South and West. We have identifications from four German Panzer Divisions, two German Infantry Divisions and one German Parachute Division. These units, spearheading the last desperate lunge, were headed straight west for key points when the Eagle Division was hurriedly ordered to stem the advance. How effectively this was done will be written in history; not alone in our Division's glorious history but in World history. The Germans actually did surround us, their radios blaring our doom. Their Commander demanded our surrender in the following impudent arrogance:

December 22nd 1944

To the U.S.A. Commander for the encircled town of Bastogne.

The Fortune of war is changing. This time the U.S.A. forces in and near Bastogne have been encircled by strong German armored units. More German armored units have crossed the river Ourthe near Ortheuville, have taken Marche and reached St. Hubert by passing through Homores-Sibrat-Tillet. Librament is in German hands.

There is only one possibility to save the encircled U.S.A. troops from total annihilation: that is the honorable surrender of the encircled town. In order to think it over a term of two hours will be granted beginning with the presentation of this note.

If this proposal should be rejected one German Artillery Corps and six heavy A.A. Battalions are ready to annihilate the U.S.A. troops in and near Bastogne. The order for firing will be given immediately after this two hour's term.

All the serious civilian losses caused by the Artillery fire would not correspond with the well known American humanity.

—The German Commander.

The German Commander received the following reply:

22 December 1944

To the German Commander: N U T S!

—The American Commander.

" 'Nuts,' " said Toye. "Gotta love that guy, McAuliffe." Around us, soldiers hooted and hollered. McAuliffe's refusal to give up encouraged us all; how fortunate that a gutsy guy like him was on watch while General Taylor was back in the States. Like the planes, his defiance reminded me that what we were doing here was about something bigger than just *us.* That we weren't folding no matter what. We were beating back everything thrown at us.

Not that his "Merry Christmas" got us in any sort of holiday spirit, thinking of Christmases back home. By dark, the wind had picked up and the windchill factor plummeted. We had navy-bean broth that night, as usual. For the first time, Winters OK'd a warming fire but the Germans must have picked up on it because an incoming mortar round pounded down, some shrapnel catching Harry Welsh below the belt. He was evacuated, went back to England, though went AWOL to later return to Easy Company.

I passed out some Lucky Strike Christmas presents, then, making sure our outpost was manned, headed for some shut-eye. All was quiet except for guys coughing, which had become as common as breathing. Some guys will tell you they heard the Germans singing "Silent Night." Maybe. I heard that song only in my head, though sound traveled so well over the snow that it's possible it was really coming from the Germans in Foy. Once in a foxhole, Bain and I would pull our "lids" of limbs and fir bows over us. A guy named Ed Thomas had concocted a more gruesome roofing system: the frozen-stiff bodies of German soldiers atop the branches. His thinking was, when shrapnel started flying, better them than us. And, hell, the krauts were already feeling no pain.

A few days later, word filtered from Bastogne that Glenn Miller's plane had gone down over the Channel in mid-December and he was missing; it was hard to imagine not hearing more fresh songs from that guy, one of the greats of big-band music. But better news came on its heels: The siege of Bastogne was finally broken. A tank battalion from Patton's 3rd Army had penetrated the German lines and rolled into town. That was wonderful. The circle was broken. We could get supplies in and wounded out. But, later, we heard that the 3rd rescued us. That cockeyed idea is phonier than a three-dollar bill. Easy Company didn't need rescuing.

One night, Joe Toye took shrapnel in the wrist when a German plane swooped low and dropped an antipersonnel bomb. It was the third time he'd been wounded since our jump into Normandy.

"Damn it," he growled. He hated getting wounded; he was

like some football team's star fullback, never wanting to stop. Never wanting to miss a single play.

"You lucky SOB," I said to him before he was taken back to an aid station in Bastogne.

"I'll be back, Malark."

Occasionally, in war, there'd be the guy who was happy to get hit; the Harvard man David Kenyon Webster, when having a bullet go cleanly through his leg in Holland, somehow had the presence of mind—and the Hollywood flare—to yell, "They *got* me!" He later said so himself. Said he'd gotten his wish: a million-dollar wound that would force him out of action. Funny, though, while Webster was back getting pampered by some sweetie-pie nurse in England, Eugene Jackson was dug in with us here at Bastogne—and had been with us in Holland—after nearly having had his ear ripped off by a mortar in Normandy. Different soldiers, you quickly learned, had different pain thresholds.

Take Toye, his arm looking like a skinned deer after that Normandy jump. Shrapnel in Holland. Now wounded here in Bastogne. You couldn't keep the guy down. And it wasn't as if he had anything to prove; every man in Easy Company respected Joe Toye for his toughness. But, remembering back to that night at the Regent Palace when I found Joe on the roof of that atrium, maybe what drove him so hard physically was the need to make up for not being, in his own mind, as "eloquent" as some of the other guys, not that I ever thought eloquence was an Easy Company trait. And not that it was his fault. Hell, your dad sends you to the coal mines when you're fifteen and you're not going to be Shakespeare; it's that simple.

It's ironic that Webster, the Harvard grad, could spin a sentence like nobody's business; he was forever writing home, regaling relatives with story after story. But you ask me whom I'd want in a foxhole with me—or, for that matter, back home, sharing a beer and a burger with me at the Liberty Grill—and I'll pick Joe Toye every damn time over a guy like Webster. You know why? Because he was always thinking beyond himself, that's why.

On New Year's Eve, I thought back to a year ago, Skip and I celebrating with the guys in England. Warm. Wild. All the food you could eat. Now, we sat in our foxholes and talked quietly. Then, with permission from Compton, just because we had ammo, we fired off six rounds of mortars to let the Germans know the worst was yet to come. A few days later, we were hunkered down when a jeep pulled up down the way, snow kicking up from its tires. It was Father Maloney. And who in the hell's with him but Joe Toye. Arm in a sling. Hadn't shaved since Adam was born. But there he was, walking across the field toward the front line. Winters saw him.

"Where you going?" he asked. "You don't have to go back to the lines."

Toye looked at him. "Gotta get back with the fellas," he said. And walked back to join the boys in Easy Company. Like the others, I just stood and watched in awe.

Lieutenant Peacock, the guy who'd busted us back in Aldbourne for smuggling in the girls in leopard-skin tights, won a thirty-day furlough back to the States. OK, Lewis Nixon won it but had the guts to stay, and Peacock was the lucky runner-up. Most of the guys were happy for him, not because he got to go home, but because they got rid of him. Nice guy, but in over his head. Meanwhile, a few guys with trench foot were sent back to England. Joe Liebgott turned quiet, morose; he'd temporarily lost his edge. In Bastogne, Toye had seen that lieutenant who'd frozen during the tank attack in Holland, the one who'd buried his head in the sand while that Tiger was ripping us; he was in an aid station, leaning against a wall, crying. Our numbers were dwindling. The only thing that kept me going was knowing I had good buddies in the foxholes down the line: Muck, Penkala, Guarnere, Toye, Hoobler—the Toccoa boys—and, of course, Buck Compton, who came to us late but was a good egg, and a sort of honorary Toccoa boy. After his being wounded in Holland, I wasn't sure we'd see him again, and I was glad he was back, though a lot of guys worried about Buck. Thought he was getting too serious. Maybe losing his edge.

We'd heard that General Taylor was now back in Bastogne. Everybody was ordered to shave within twenty-four hours and to remove their boots once a day and massage their feet. I refused the foot order, having tried and found it only made things worse. Come to think of it, I refused the shaving order, too, as did most of us.

We'd heard from guys in Bastogne that the 101st was making headlines back home. We'd broken the German siege. Beaten the odds. All at a time when newspapers were looking for good hero stories and citizens looking for hope. But, believe me, we soldiers in those Bastogne foxholes weren't feeling particularly heroic. What we mainly felt was cold. Our beards grew longer, our patience shorter. The snow resumed, now halfway to our knees. It would snow again every day for a week. Somehow it didn't seem to bother the German planes, which were harassing us day and night. We had been on the front lines for fifteen days in Belgium, on top of seventy in Holland and twenty-three in Normandy. A total of 108 days, not that anybody was counting. In war, you count days the way prisoners mark walls. Will this ever end? Will we ever make it out alive? Will I get home to be with Bernice and pick blackberries? Will Skip marry Faye Tanner and live happily ever after? Such questions rattled around in your mind here and there, between the short spurts of combat and the much longer nights.

On January 2, we headed out into Jack's Woods to flush out any German soldiers before our inevitable attack on Foy. Before leaving, standing around a warming fire, we got to know a seven-man bazooka team from the 10th Armored Division that had joined us. We worked our way through the woods to the east, where the forest came to the edge of the Foy–Bizory road. We scooted across, knowing we couldn't probably be seen from German outposts in Foy. We worked our way north with hardly any opposition. The worst problem was heavy snow piling up in the brush.

Suddenly, an ear-piercing sound split the air: "screaming meemies," like huge mortars and projectiles tumbling through the air, end over end, making an eerie whirling noise. They overshot us, their bark worse than their bite.

Darkness was setting in. Defensive positions were set for the night. I didn't see it, but later a German soldier came roaring through the woods on horseback, apparently like something out of "The Legend of Sleepy Hollow." Scared the hell out of everybody there. He saw our men, probably wet his pants, pulled a one-eighty-degree turn, and headed back. Don Hoobler, a likable kid from Ohio, coolly pumped three rounds into the soldier's back. The German fell off, and the horse ran off. Hoobler, a good friend of mine, was quite proud of himself.

We dug in as best we could, not easy in the snow. Buck Compton moved from foxhole to foxhole to check on us. "Guys doin' OK?" he'd say. Or, "Keep moving those toes."

The frontline machine-gun positions were in such heavy thicket that Burr Smith was actually exchanging banter with the krauts. Suddenly, *crack*. A gun went off nearby and a soldier screamed. One of ours. Hoobler. A guy I'd known since our runs up Currahee. He had been fiddling with a Browning 45mm pistol—not a Luger as some thought—in his right-hand pocket and apparently accidentally shot himself in the leg. He was squirming in the snow, the blood gushing dangerously fast from his right leg. He'd severed a main artery.

"Help me, help me, oh, God, help me," he cried.

A 1st Platoon medic bent over and tried to stop the bleeding. "Need help. Gotta get this man to an aid station." Two guys hauled him off, leaving a trail of blood in the snow. Later, we heard he died shortly after arriving at the aid station. Bled to death.

In the quiet of the woods that followed, you couldn't help thinking fatalistic thoughts. You figured the law of averages was going to stay with you only so long in combat. And that you were living and fighting on borrowed time.

Late the next afternoon, Winters pulled us out of our advanced position; he wanted us back in our old spots, perched in the woods overlooking Foy. At least part of the concern was that we had no reserves to fill the flanks; if Jerries got past us, we'd be fighting on three sides. Not good.

The light started fading. We were trudging back to our old position—eighteen Easy guys and half a dozen guys from the bazooka team that had joined us—when we had to cross a narrow country lane. Looking back, I think the Germans might have seen us heading back to our positions in the woods because just as we arrived, so did a shelling like we'd never seen before or would see after. The Jerries started pounding us with big ones, probably 170s and 88s, as if they'd known exactly where we were heading. The shells rained down with the thunder of freight trains. *Ka-boom, ka-boom, ka-boom!* One after another.

"Incoming!" Compton yelled. "G'down! Take cover!" I found a hole in a hurry and tucked my head as if praying, which I did, too. Rod Bain piled in next to me. Around us, people were yelling, diving into foxholes and shell holes. Or, if desperate, cowering behind trees.

The shells were set to explode on contact, creating "tree bursts" that flung shrapnel and knifelike shards of wood in all directions. Pines snapped in half and slammed to the snow with thumps, limbs flying crazily. I'd seen logging crews in action back home, but nothing like this chaos of falling trees. The ground exploded, dirt shooting up like geysers. Guys were running around, desperately looking for cover. For a moment, I was a twelve-year-old kid back in Oregon. *"Bob, Donnie, get up, get up! Fire's comin'."*

"Get down! Find some cover!" Compton kept yelling. The bazooka team from the 10th Armored scurried for foxholes but none were to be had. Too late. *Ka-boom!* Their bodies were flung into the air, twisting and turning before landing contorted in the snow.

Bain and I winced as the shells kept coming like oversized machine-gun fire. I'd been through a lot since Normandy, but nothing as intense, as loud, as constantly dooming as this. When the shells hit, they literally bounced you up.

Ka-boom, ka-boom, ka-boom! The shelling continued. Bain was curled up in the fetal position, hands over his head. Outside, barely audible above the noise from the attack, I heard voices of soldiers: Someone yelling to take cover. Someone moaning. Someone yelling, "I'm hit."

Ka-boom, ka-boom, ka-boom!

Then, suddenly, quiet. As quickly as the attack began, it ended, the sound of shells replaced by the sound of the *shelled*: Bain and I barely heard it far in the distance. "Gotta get up . . . gotta get up."

It sounded like Joe Toye. I popped my head out of the fox-hole and looked around for Buck Compton, for orders. That's when we heard what sounded like Toye again. "Gotta get up . . . gotta get up . . ."

Hearing that, Guarnere, Toye's best friend, scrambled out of his foxhole like a madman, heading for his pal. He was playing right into the krauts' hands: hit 'em with a barrage, allow them a little time to go after their wounded, then hit 'em again. But there was no stopping Guarnere. Bill got to Joe and was dragging him, by his two arms, back to a fox-hole, leaving a streak of blood in the snow. Joe was missing a leg.

"Ge' back, Bill," people were yelling. "Take cover!" But he wouldn't leave Toye by himself. "Bill, find cover!" He glanced over his shoulder, spotting a foxhole. He was almost—

Ka-boom, ka-boom!

Guarnere and Toye disappeared in a hail of dirt, snow, shrapnel, and tree shards. The earth shook.

Ka-boom, ka-boom, ka-boom!

Another soldier screamed. Finally, the barrage stopped again. It was eerily silent, broken by the panicked voice of Buck Compton.

"Medic! Medic!" He'd seen what the rest of us would ~on see: Toye and Guarnere, flattened in the snow, both missing legs, wrapped together in a bloody tangle.

Compton started running back toward the command post, completely exposed to incoming fire. A couple of our guys sprang out of foxholes, tackled him, and dragged him to cover. He'd seen enough pain and suffering. Not just in this moment. But in all the moments that added up to a guy not being able to take it anymore.

I looked out of my foxhole and wished I hadn't. More than a dozen soldiers were bleeding in the snow. Cries for help rose from all over the woods. Safe or not to be in the open, guys popped out of foxholes and went to Guarnere, Toye, and the others. I was huddling around Joe. Our medic, Roe, was tying a tourniquet around what was left of Joe's leg, just below the knee. He'd already gotten a good hit of morphine; Guarnere would be next. The look on Joe's face was the same look I'd seen in him that night I'd talked him off the roof at the Regent, a cross between *I don't wanna live* and *I don't wanna die,* with a touch of *I'm letting Easy down.* Anguish. As if he'd somehow failed not only himself, but all of us.

"Take it easy, Joe, you're going to be OK," I said.

A jeep had come up from the rear and wound its way through the trees. We put Toye's stretcher sideways across the front. "Malark, gimme a cigarette," he said, breathing hard.

I just looked at him and kept saying how it was going to be OK, even though I didn't think it was. How can it be OK when a guy who's already been wounded three times is hit for a fourth and, if he makes it, is going to be hobbling on one leg the rest of his life?

I put the cigarette in his mouth. He took a drag and blew out the smoke.

"God, what's a guy gotta do to die, Malark?" he said.

I sniffed and looked away, then back. "I dunno, Joe. I dunno."

Guarnere was still behind us, grimacing in pain, meaning two of the toughest guys in the unit were now fighting for life. Around us, guys stood around with the proverbial thousand-yard stare in their eyes. The once-white snow was tinted with dirt and splotched with blood.

"Malark, give us a hand over here," Roe said while working on Guarnere.

There was no time to grieve. The war had to go on.

Or did it?

One shot.

That's all it would take, I figured as I warmed my hands around the campfire with a few other shivering soldiers a few days later. It happened all the time, these "accidents." Why not now? Why not here? Why not me?

I stared at the embers, stretched out my fingers, then closed my hands when they got too hot. Hell, everyone found their way out of this, whether intentional or not. Hoobler and Ranney—shots to the leg. One dies, one doesn't, but both got their get-out-of-jail-free cards. Toye and Guarnere—legs blown to bits. Buck—blown to bits, too, but just in a different way—emotionally. Not his fault. The guy busted his butt for us. The last time I saw him, he was like a ghost. His eyes seemed to look right through me, as if I weren't even there and he was seeing something else completely.

That was two days earlier. I put my right hand onto the holster, then around the cold stock of the P38. I thought I was a pretty tough kid, growing up in a hardscrabble place like Astoria. I got tougher on Mount Currahee. And on that road to Atlanta, lugging a sixty-five-pound mortar 118 miles. And jumping into the darkness of Normandy. And surviving seventy days in the muck and mutton of Holland. But standing around that fire, you realize the price for surviving is seeing so many around you *not* survive—and having to stuff that pain in your musette bag every friggin' day and keep walking, with so little hope of ever getting to whatever's at the end. And you think, *Maybe they're the lucky SOBs.* The ones who are suddenly gone, not that I'd wish death on anyone. Like that telegram my grandfather had sent from Denver when my uncle Bob was dying: *If he is to pass at this time he begs of you all . . . not to grieve unduly for he will be released from suffering and at peace.*

Once, I asked Skip about swimming the Niagara. He and his pals had started about ten miles above the waterfalls. It was nearly a mile across with a swift current. They knew that to get across they'd wind up at least a few miles downstream. Anyway, about four or five miles from the falls, he said, was a point-of-no-return sign. If you weren't able to get your boat or body out of the river by this point, your fate was sealed. You were going over the falls, period. And staring at those embers, that's exactly how I felt right now: beyond the point of no return. Helpless to do anything but relax and go over the edge.

I looked at the fire, careful not to look in the eyes of the men standing around me, the other survivors. I'd lost eight Toccoa buddies since those days in Georgia, not even counting the busted-up ones such as Toye and Guarnere. Slowly, my right forefinger curled around the icy pistol's trigger.

I wanted to leave it all behind: the cold, the eerie quiet of the forest before you heard the whistle of a shell, and the helpless look in Joe Toye's eyes when he'd said, "What's a guy gotta do to die, Malark?" Above all, I think, for the first time I realized that this war had no end and that I'd never smell late-summer blackberries or see Bernice again unless I—

"Sergeant Malarkey?"

The voice came from behind, scaring the hell out of me. I slid the gun back in its holster. It was some soldier who'd arrived by jeep.

"Winters sent me, Sergeant. There's someone back in the woods who wants to see you."

Buck Compton looked nothing like the soldier who'd walked off the line a few days before. Well-starched Class A uniform. Hair combed. He was taking quick drags on a cigarette. His driver was waiting for him in a jeep.

"I've been reassigned, Malark," he said. "Some desk job in Paris. Director of athletics and entertainment or something." He'd wanted to stay with the company but Winters wouldn't allow it.

"That's great, Buck," I said.

"Dick said I could come say good-bye."

"I'm glad you did. I'm happy for you."

He looked around. "Don, there's something I need to know." He paused and looked beyond me, back toward the woods where I'd just made fresh tracks in the snow. Back to where the others were.

"What, uh—what do the other guys think of me?"

I couldn't lie. "They think you're a hell of an officer, Buck."

"Really?"

"Really. They wish you the best. Honest."

He nodded, his lips pursed a bit. "Thanks, Malark."

He looked at me and saluted. I saluted back. And we left to go to the different places we each needed to be.

13
BURYING IT DEEP WITHIN

Bastogne
January 4–January 19, 1945

I didn't cry after learning Skip Muck was dead. That would come later. Much later. Not that it didn't hurt. Hell, I'd never felt pain so deep. He was like my brother. No, closer than my brother. But by January 9, when he'd died in a shelling about one hundred yards east of where I was, I was too mentally numb to really react. Too tired. I didn't sleep a wink for two nights after Roe broke the news to me. And after seeing Toye and Guarnere carted off, and Compton leaving, it was like dumping ice on a guy who was already frozen stiff.

But the main reason I didn't crumble at his death is I couldn't. That wasn't allowed. With Compton gone, I realized I had to step up and lead. After Guarnere went down, Winters had promoted me to permanent sergeant status.

Now, Buck was gone. From day one, you're taught that the good of the whole is more important that just *you*. That you can't let your emotions get in the way of the task at hand. So like a doctor who deals with pain and death each day, you just bury it somewhere deep down inside, thinking it'll go away on its own.

If I'd put that bullet through my leg or gone to pieces when Toye and Guarnere had been wounded, or when Skip had died, what would it have done to the rest of these guys? Hell, we were all at the breaking point. Hanging on to whatever shred of resolve we still had in us. And if a few of us didn't stand up and lead as if we were going to somehow survive this cold and outlast this last-gasp push by the krauts, what would happen to Easy Company? You might as well bury us all beneath one giant headstone, etched with the words THE S.O.B.S QUIT. Hardly a fitting legacy to those left behind, including my uncles.

Not that I thought this all out back when it was happening, back when I heard the crunch of feet in the snow and turned to see Roe coming my way. I could tell by the look on his face that this wasn't a social visit.

"Malark, I'm sorry, but it's Skip," he said. "He's dead. Penkala, too."

I simply sat on the edge of a slit trench like a man who'd been out in the cold too long. Numb. My brain told my mouth to speak but it was like the words were frozen in place.

"How'd . . . it . . . happen?" I asked, my voice but a whisper.

" 'Bout a hundred yards down the line. A major shelling. Muck and Penkala were caught out in the open, then finally found a hole. George Luz had been scurrying around during the blitz, too. Muck and Penkala yelled for him to get in their foxhole."

Roe paused. I kind of nodded, rocked forward and backward a bit. Put my hands over my face, fingers as numb from the cold as my brain from the news.

"Luz is down on the snow, snaking his way toward them, and—boom—direct hit on the foxhole. Shell found them as if it had eyes."

I looked away, toward nothing. Thought of Faye Tanner back in Tonawanda.

I didn't need to think on that one long; later, I'd hear that beyond a shredded sleeping bag and a few body parts, there wasn't much to see. I shook my head sideways. That wasn't Skip Muck back there in that foxhole. Skip Muck was sitting on the floor of the PX with me, listening to the Mills Brothers sing "Paper Doll" on the jukebox. He was getting my food for me when my legs had given out on the march to Atlanta. He was swimming the damn Niagara River at night, a thought that made me want to laugh and cry at the same time, the crazy fool.

I did neither.

"Thanks, Roe. I'm fine."

He reached into his pocket. "Here," he said, pressing the cross of some broken rosary beads in my hand. "He'd want you to have it."

I held that cross in my hands for who knows how long, frozen like a statue. A few hours later, Roe came to see me again. I was staring off at nothing, still holding that cross.

"Malark, uh, Winters wants to know if you want to come back and spend a couple of days with him at headquarters. Help out there, ya know. Be a runner."

Sounded inviting. But I looked around at the others, heads bowed, some of their eyes red, crying over Skip. First time I'd ever seen that in war. Everybody in tears. Everybody but me. I was a staff sergeant now. We had no officers left. I was in charge. And staff sergeants can't lead by sipping hot coffee a quarter mile back from the line. Or crying. Who cares how fast the current's going; you gotta swim the friggin' river.

"Tell him thanks, but I'll stay put."

"Sure, Malark? You could use a break. Everyone needs a breather now and then."

"I'm OK, Roe," I said, nodding as if to convince myself.

Easy Company was through playing games with the German soldiers at Foy. Other companies, like F, had attacked Foy and gotten pretty badly chewed up. The Germans had been bringing in trucks and tanks. But, after a couple of days of rest, we figured it was now or never. We'd swept the woods left and right. It was time to head straight in.

Besides the Jerries, two things worried me about this attack. First, there were no two ways about it: At some point, we were going to have to charge across an open field of snow, a soldier's worst nightmare against an enemy that's entrenched with buildings and trees to protect them. Second, a guy who'd hardly seen any combat, Capt. Norman Dike, would be leading the assault. Dike was Compton's replacement, some nose-in-the-air Yaley who knew someone high up. He spooked everyone. He was Sobel without the toughness. In the blasts that got Guarnere and Toye, Dike had scurried off like a scared rabbit. But, in war, sometimes you gotta dance with who brung ya, as they say.

Winters was feeding Dike instructions like a coach to a rookie quarterback. We moved out. Our covering fire opened up. A smoke barrage was laid down in front of the buildings the Germans were using for defensive positions. We headed across the field. The 3rd Platoon went in on a frontal attack and were in an orchard about a hundred yards from the buildings when the smoke lifted. They were taking heavy fire and casualties. We flanked in from the west. First was in reserve and would later come in to help 3rd.

I spotted one of the machine-gun positions. "Fire mortars!" I yelled to my mortarman, some replacement I hardly knew.

We were standing in the open, alongside a rock fence structure while I pointed out the gun I had seen. The mortarman crouched to set the tube.

Ch-ch-ch-ch-ch-ch-ch-ch-ch-ch-ch. He was ripped by eight rounds of machine-gun fire. Not dead, but seriously wounded. Still, there was no way in hell we could get him out of there until we had Foy in our hands. He bled to death.

By now, I'd later learn, our attack was in total disarray. Dike had frozen behind a haystack. Flat-out refused to lead the charge. Winters was going nuts on the radio, trying to get Dike's butt in gear, trying to get him to move the men forward. Finally, Winters had had it; he put Speirs in charge, the same Speirs who'd been rumored to have mowed down the German POWs and once killed one of his own sergeants. But, as it turned out, a wise replacement for Dike, who was wetting his pants. I never totally respected Speirs because of the times he'd gone too far with his tommy gun, but he knew how to lead in combat and always was fair with me.

Our platoon continued to work our way in. We found cover behind an outbuilding. I heard German gunfire from an adjacent outbuilding, apparently coming from a single soldier. Breathing heavily, I looked at the corporal next to me.

"I'll get him," I said, my back to the building. I inched sideways, getting ready to spin around the corner and open fire.

"Sarge, you're in charge of this outfit," the corporal said. "I'll go."

Reluctantly, I nodded a yes. He stuck his head around the corner of the building. *Pfffft.* A bullet killed him instantly, a yard from where I stood. Angered, I hopped over him, dashed around the corner, and opened fire with my tommy gun. There was a German soldier in a barn window, obviously the guy who'd just killed that corporal. I mowed him down, then came up on the barn itself. I poked my head inside. My heart was pounding.

"Anybody else in here need killing?" I yelled. No movement. I looked around to make sure nobody was hiding, then relaxed, assured I was safe. I saw the soldier I'd just killed, sprawled on the barn floor, helmet off. Two or three bullets had bloodied his chest, which, against his gray uniform, looked more crimson than red. Damn, he looked so young. I bent over and found his soldier's record—the Germans called them pay books—and glanced at it. Holy mother of God, this kid was only sixteen years old. Looking back, it was like the time as a kid I'd shot what I thought was my first quail. Only, when I ran to where it had nose-dived into some tall grass, I realized it wasn't a quail after all, but a robin. I felt like two cents.

The kid was probably part of Hitler Youth. He'd had no choice in all this. Just swept up in a madman's pursuit of evil. I looked at his face, eyes fixed forever. A face that I wouldn't forget. Not the next day. Not the next month. Not ever. I tucked his pay book in my pocket and moved on.

As I moved up to the wall of a house, I realized the 3rd

Platoon had already gotten there because the place was littered with the dead and dying. We surged forward, Easy Company and others of the 506th, dumping everything we had on them: M1s, tommy guns, bazookas, light machine guns, mortars, and grenades. Resistance was strong. By now it was house-to-house fighting. Snipers, well placed in high positions, were picking off our guys right and left. Finally, Shifty Powers spotted them and opened fire with great success.

In one house, as I rushed in, a fellow American soldier was coming out. It was Eugene Brown, my old classmate from the University of Oregon, the guy whom I'd twice forgotten to salute at Toccoa. I wasn't any more formal here. "Hi, Gene," I said.

He didn't seem to mind; combat zones lend themselves to informality. Plus, I think he glanced at the stripes on my shoulder. "Malark, great to see you!" he responded.

Whatever Germans were still alive were hightailing it east, toward Noville. The few Tiger tanks followed. The Germans, it turned out, had only been fighting a rearguard action to cover a withdrawal to Noville, behind Foy. Finally, after more than three weeks, Foy was ours. At least for now. The Germans would counterattack the next day, but the 3rd Platoon would hold them off.

As we regrouped for the push to Noville, word spread about Dike freezing up in the heat of battle. It didn't surprise me. From the get-go, I'd been unimpressed with the midlevel officers and their inability to lead when they needed to. It was the only weakness in the 506th, this revolving door of guys who had no business being in charge. Sobel. Evans. Peacock. Dike. Compton's lieutenant who turned to mush in

Holland. A couple of rookies at Hell's Corner who Winters had to take out because they had no idea where our machine-gun positions were in relation to our defensive posture. Was it because the ROTC programs back in the States didn't do a better job of weeding them out? Because too many guys just didn't have their hearts in it, just wanted an extra fifty bucks a month? Or because of politics, some higher-up's "golden boy"—Dike comes to mind—getting foisted on soldiers who deserved better?

Hard to say. All I know is that, at times, Easy Company succeeded not because of the leadership but in spite of it. Oh, we had a few good ones: Harry Welsh, Bob Brewer, even Ron Speirs, despite his "killer" reputation. First Lt. Thomas Meehan, who'd taken over for Sobel, was a good man, but his plane had gone down in Normandy. Dick Winters, who replaced him, was a glowing exception, too; he had that uncommon blend of smarts and concern for the guys. Cool as a cucumber when the pressure was on. Fair to all. And comfortable enough being Dick Winters that you never got the idea he had to stomp on the rest of us to boost his own battle-scarred ego. And he was absolutely willing to go through whatever we went through; hell, I always thought he was happiest when he was with us in the foxholes. I don't think he did ever completely adjust to being in the rear, out of the action. He wanted to be out there with us. And, in a sense, he was.

Dike was permanently relieved of his duties. Speirs was put in command of Easy Company. For now, Easy Company was as exhausted as we'd ever been. Though we slept inside actual structures that night for the first time since Mourmelon, about a month ago, the cold seemed more intense. The next morning, we moved out, heading for

Noville, a larger village just down the road that had been our objective since we'd first dug in, in those Bastogne woods. A light snow fell.

Noville required another risky approach in an open field. It was January 14. We moved out through the snow. Meanwhile, the 1st Battalion advanced far to our left, being pummeled by German 88s. We soon had problems of our own: Machine guns from Noville had opened on us. Speirs set up a couple of machine guns in response. With each burst of fire, we'd advance a little more across a small stream and into position for a morning assault. A horse, its legs shattered by a shell fragment, stood in a nearby field. One of our noncoms put it out of its misery.

Meanwhile, our misery continued. That night, January 14, with no enemy fire, we tucked up under a deep shoulder of land and waited to attack in the morning. It was, some would remember, the coldest night of the war. We shivered through the night, having got plenty sweaty moving to this point. At one point, Winters considered just attacking in the darkness rather than freeze in it, but decided against it for fear we'd shoot our own men.

Early in the morning, Carwood Lipton and a radioman crept forward to assess the situation. He found knocked-out Sherman tanks and lots of bodies of Allied soldiers, frozen like plastic army men, the dead of a battle from nearly a month earlier.

We started the assault at dawn. The village was ours by noon; resistance had been lighter than expected. Now it was on to Rachamps, a tiny village about three kilometers beyond, the last of three objectives we'd had when we arrived here. The 11th Armored Division joined us on our flank, one of the few times we'd have the luxury of such bulk. We moved north on high ground and found ourselves looking down into a treeless basin with the village nestled amid white fields at the bottom. The snow on the village's front door dipped into a giant bowl, and it was decided we could find good cover if we could just get to the far end of that bowl. But that meant, of course, an approach in a wide-open field.

We started moving forward in snow nearly two feet deep. A soldier's best friend is cover and we had none. It was a strange feeling of vulnerability. But the German garrison must have been apprehensive about our approach. They lobbed some 88s our way, not exploding shells but armor-piercing, and all were too long or too short. Other resistance was light, almost as if they were giving in to the inevitable. We started running to find cover behind fences and buildings. I looked up from behind a wall. A Belgian farmer was standing in the window of a farmhouse, frantically waving and pointing to the cellar of the house. He held up two fingers and pointed down. A pair of Germans were downstairs.

A handful of us moved forward. I opened the back door and could see the stairs to the basement.

"Comeinzeout!" I yelled.

No response. I threw a grenade down. *Boom.* A dog scurried upstairs. I yelled again. Again, no response. I opened fire with a tommy gun as I started down the stairs and finally heard some German words. Finally, two officers slunk up the stairs, one waving a white handkerchief.

I don't remember who interrogated them, but they said they were told they were supposed to fight to the last man or a German 88 unit was going to level the town, including them. We took sixty-five prisoners that day and didn't lose a man. Late in the day, the two officers were being held in a village barn. Sgt. Earl Hale and a rifleman, Joe Liebgott, were guarding them. One of the prisoners sprang on Hale, slitting his throat. Liebgott killed both. Somehow, Hale survived.

As did Easy Company after nearly a month in this frozen hell. Later that evening, word came down that the 17th Airborne would be relieving us, or whatever was left of us. We had arrived at Bastogne on December 19 with about 120 men; between death, wounds, trench foot, and guys who just couldn't take it anymore, we now had about 60. Among my friends: Muck and Hoobler, dead. Toye, Guarnere, Gordon, Smith, and Perconte, wounded. Compton, gone.

In a letter from Bernice, she'd asked what it was like for me in war. I wrote back, saying, among other things, this:

When we were surrounded I sometimes felt we would never pull out of it. Generally, I was confident—in spite of the suffering. Can you imagine, honey, living in a foxhole with ice on the side and hanging from an improvised roof? Outside the snow was up to your knees. We had to wrap our feet in burlap bags to keep them from freezing—even then, many of (the men) had toes that wouldn't function. I can remember how my hands would freeze to my tommy gun.

The fact that you're still alive is the only important thing. I know you don't know what it is to face death. It's the most punishing experience you can imagine. And when you're fighting you're going through it 24 hours a day. It's hard, darling, to walk into those Kraut tanks, machine guns, artillery, etc when you know you've got so much to live for. It takes a lot of that stuff called 'guts' that too damn few men have. Having been as lucky as I am, I begin to feel that I'm a fugitive from the law of averages, which isn't good. This war is hell all right.

Then, in the same letter, I obviously remembered the low point of that hell. Skip's death.

> *How would you feel if you were walking down the street with a friend and suddenly she was blown into a thousand pieces? My best friend was killed at my side, the greatest little guy I've ever known. I was more broken up than I've ever been in my life but there's no turnin' back—keep drivin'—and for five days after we kept attackin'.*
>
> *Each day more of my friends would leave for a better world. That's a sample of what I've been doing. I could never describe the terror that strikes you when you're under those terrific artillery barrages when the exploding steel seemingly pounds you into the ground and makes your head reel, your ears pop, and your heart stop beating. I would tell you a lot more about legs and arms, faces, eyes, etc. that are no longer usable. That's the kind of a life I know—not an existence of a human being [but] the life of a madman.*

In Bastogne, though, the end had finally come. Once Rachamps was secured and we had the POWs together, I was invited to one of the farmhouses whose family had not fled. It was the first time I'd been indoors, in a warm building, in a month. A warm fire was burning in a huge rock fireplace, and I stood in front of those flames and soaked them up like a hungry man who hadn't eaten in weeks, as if I'd forgotten how good a fire could feel. The smell of a fire always takes me back to those summer evenings, as a kid, cooking crawdads or fish over the flames on the Nehalem River.

When Skip came to visit, we were going to do that. We were going to catch sea-run cutthroat and bake them over the flames and drink beer. And I was going to see his old haunts in upstate New York. Meet Faye, the girl whom I felt I almost knew because Skip had talked so much about her. Maybe be in the wedding.

But that knock on the door in Mourmelon had changed everything.

14

LETTERS FROM TWO WOMEN

France, Belgium, Germany
January 20, 1945–May 8, 1945

Combat pushes so much adrenaline through your
veins that once you stop fighting, once that rush is over, you
come down harder than the morning after an all-night
binge. Doubly hard when, arriving by truck at a place in
France called Haguenau, you see the 1st Platoon boys arrive
and remember he's not with the outfit anymore. Of Skip's
1st Platoon, only eleven of the forty men were still with the
unit.

For Easy Company, Haguenau, about 160 miles southeast
of Bastogne, was a place of transition. We were joined by a
bunch of replacement soldiers, wet-behind-the-ears types
who knew the war was winding down but wanted to get in a
few licks before the last shot was fired. Some were the real
deal. Others just wanted to send a picture back home to con-

vince everybody that they were a war hero. Still others were a bit of both, like a kid named Hank Jones, a second lieutenant fresh out of West Point who was both cocky and totally green; looked like the kid on your block back home who sold *Grit* magazines door-to-door.

"Sir," he said when I first met him. "I'm here to be your assistant and you will leave for a while and come back as my assistant." I liked his pluck, but he'd confused me with Carwood Lipton, who he assumed was going to be up for a battlefield commission.

The idea of being replaced did, frankly, have some appeal to it; by now, I was so tired my mind seemed in a fog. But I wasn't quitting.

"Thanks, Jones," I said. "But I'm sticking right here with the Second Platoon."

Beyond the fresh faces, we had a few guys rejoin us who'd been wounded in Normandy or Holland and were now recovered. Among them was Webster, the Harvard man so busy polishing his Bobcat badge that he didn't realize that damn near everybody else was now an Eagle Scout. Or dead. Or, like Toye and Guarnere, lying in some hospital back in England trying to figure out how in the hell to walk on one leg for the rest of their lives.

Webster, who'd taken a single bullet cleanly through the leg in Holland, showed up in Haguenau with the pep of a kid being dropped off at a birthday party—and not smart enough to figure out the rest of us weren't much in a partying mood. He kept asking where so-and-so was. And guys kept telling him: "dead . . . lost a leg . . . took a shot in the neck . . . froze his friggin' feet off. . . ."

I looked at Webster in his fresh uniform, then headed off to find the portable showers that I'd heard had been trucked in for us. A shower felt good, even if the water wasn't exactly stateside hot. But as I stood there, ignoring the "Hurry it up, pal" impatience of guys in line, I let that water wash over my face, wishing I could wash Bastogne off me like it was nothing more than salmon blood on my hands from a day hauling the seines on the Columbia.

I closed my eyes and there I was, sitting on the edge of that foxhole, Roe's words almost in slow motion: *Malark, I'm sorry, but it's Skip. . . .* Over and over.

Since Bastogne, I'd learned that Muck would never have been in such a vulnerable position had another unit—some non-101st unit—done its job that day and occupied some settlements west of Foy. But they failed, which meant scrubbing the very mission that had moved the 1st Platoon to the front. In other words, Skip shouldn't have been sitting in that foxhole at that moment.

I toweled off my face. Yeah, Haguenau was a place of transition. You sensed the war in Europe was winding down, as if the Germans were just lobbing a few shells here and there to remind us that they weren't scampering home with their tail between their legs. But, suddenly, with time to think, you started wondering if it would ever really be over.

Haguenau sat on the Moder River. I'm sure it was beautiful in the spring and summer; for now, in mid-February and in midwar, it was battered buildings connected by muddy streets. The Germans had launched a diversionary operation in this region to draw American troops out of the Bastogne area. A few of their soldiers, probably not more than a squad, were milling about across the river, not more than a hundred yards from us.

With the 2nd Platoon still without an officer, I was, as a staff sergeant, in charge. Our headquarters was a large house owned by a dentist who, like lots of dentists in Europe, had his practice as part of his home. He was also the mayor of Haguenau. And reportedly a Nazi who'd fled pretty fast when he heard Americans were coming to town. Without much to do one day, we blew open a safe in his house, but all we found was some coins, loose jewelry, and two stamp albums. I gave the coins and jewelry to guys in the company; later, I sent the stamp albums home to my parents.

At Haguenau, I got some mail: a letter from Bernice. We were talking marriage by now, though I kept getting the idea I was more excited about it than she was. "Life without you," I had written in January from Bastogne, "wouldn't be worth living." Later, I wrote about having no chance to grieve for those you've lost.

> *I am sorry, darling, that you allowed yourself to be so assured that I was soon to strike the shores of the good old U.S.A. I know how hard it is on you, emotionally. With me, it isn't so bad for the army doesn't allow you to display or harbor emotions. It's the constant suppressing of them that brings about the psychological changes in men that people notice in returning veterans. Personally, that doesn't worry me for I'll probably be overly emotional in my return to you.*

I also got a letter from Joe Toye. Pretty much one-syllable words, which always bothered Joe but not me. Hell, it wasn't how you said something, it was that you took the time to say it. Anyway, they'd cut his leg off within a couple of days of his getting it ripped to shreds at Bastogne. Then again in

England. Then, back in the States, he got gangrene and had to have it cut again. "Tonight," he said, "they're cuttin' it for the fourth time, and if it's not successful, I've already been told that's it. I die." Guarnere, we heard, was recovering but had lost his leg.

By now, Easy Company had lost its enthusiasm for war; it didn't help hearing that dozens of our boys had been massacred by the krauts someplace north of Bastogne called Malmédy. I was slipping into a bit more cynicism than usual. When General Maxwell Taylor, back in the war zone after conveniently missing a tiny skirmish called the Battle of the Bulge, came through for an inspection, I mentally rolled my eyes.

"Sergeant, were you wearing your helmet when it was hit?" he asked, looking at a helmet with a chunk missing after I'd taken a bullet from that P-47 that the krauts had apparently stolen and used to dive-bomb us.

I wanted to shake my head and say, "What do you think?" Instead I said, "Yes, sir."

"Well, in that case you can continue wearing it."

The incident showed how little the pencil-pushing brass knew about frontline duty. Anyone with a helmet with that kind of damage wouldn't have had a friggin' head if the helmet hadn't been on his head when he was hit. I continued to wear it. And would have even if he'd told me I couldn't.

When word came down that we were going to send a patrol across the Moder River and bring back a few Germans who could cough up some info, nobody leapt to their feet. Nobody, that is, except Jones. I was going, but later word came down from Lt. Dick Winters that he wanted Jones, the West Point rookie, to replace me.

That was fine by me. I wasn't hurt, I was relieved, and so tired that I wouldn't have been a good choice to go anyway. My assignment was, along with Speirs, to provide covering fire from the second floor of a house. The mission was like a deadly game of checkers. We got two of their guys as prisoners and lost two guys; Sgt. Bill Kiehn was killed outright and Eugene Jackson got hammered by the wooden handle of a potato masher.

Poor Jackson. He's the guy who'd taken a large fragment from a mortar in the side of his head in Normandy, then shown up before the Holland jump as if nothing had happened. Now, he was fighting for what little life was left in him. They'd dragged him back across the river, into our headquarters house, but everybody in the room knew he wasn't going to make it. And he didn't. He kept calling over and over for his "mama" to help him. He died as they tried to get him to a military hospital. Of shock—that's what I heard. He was only nineteen, among those soldiers so anxious to get in that he'd lied about his age back when he was sixteen.

The patrol had, in relation to other stuff we'd faced since the jump into Normandy, been pretty small potatoes. But afterward, Jones seemed sufficiently impressed that war was a big boys' ball game. Watching Jackson die, Jones's face was white as a ghost. He remained with the company for a short time, then was transferred to a higher echelon. Rumor had it that the war would soon end, and the West Pointers were being protected to staff peacetime armies.

A few days later, command sent word that they wanted another patrol, needed a few more German soldiers. By then, it had turned colder; a thin layer of ice coated the Moder. Could we have sent that patrol and got those prisoners?

Sure. But Winters didn't want to risk it. He sent in a report that wasn't really true but wasn't really false; it said something like "Unable to secure prisoners. All our men safe." You never talk about these things at the time, but I think, like us all, he was still a little numb from Bastogne and yet finally hopeful that, if we were careful, we might actually get out of this alive. The first patrol, in my mind, was a waste of two good men. I'm glad Dick made it our last patrol.

Our moods rose. Winters was promoted to major. Some late Christmas presents started arriving, candy and cookies and stuff. My aunt Claudia in Portland was good about sending food, occasionally some Norwegian sardines. That smell would permeate any place we'd open them, though they'd get wolfed down in minutes. Ed Stein, who was Jewish, kept telling me, "Sarge, wait until you taste the strawberries my mother is sending." Some Jewish delicacy, and a dish that I'm sure is good. When fresh. But it includes sour cream, and after weeks—hell, maybe months—en route I took one whiff and headed for open air. Looking over my shoulder, I saw Stein was savoring each bite.

In the last few days in Haguenau, I started looking forward to a train, not a truck, ride to Mourmelon. I thought a lot about Faye Tanner back in New York, who had, by now, heard there was no need to wait for Skip to come home. With time to think again about something beyond combat—about being patient and getting home and those who wait—I tumbled Milton's "On His Blindness" around in my head:

> When I consider how my light is spent
> Ere half my days, in this dark world and wide,

And that one talent which is death to hide
Lodged with me useless, though my soul more bent

To serve therewith my Maker, and present
My true account, lest He returning chide,—
Doth God exact day-labour, light denied?
I fondly ask:—But Patience, to prevent

That murmur, soon replies: God doth not need
Either man's work, or His own gifts, who best
Bear His mild yoke, they serve Him best. His state
Is kingly; thousands at His bidding speed
And post o'er land and ocean without rest:—
They also serve who only stand and wait.

Returning to Mourmelon, after three weeks in Haguenau, I kept putting it off. There were, after all, other things to consider, like who in the hell had looted our barracks while we were gone. We had stored all our belongings in the center of our barracks living room. When the door opened, all we saw was a huge pile of clothing nearly reaching to the ceiling. We'd been professionally looted, we suspected by some air force rear-echelon folks who'd arrived after we left for Bastogne. Gone were all our souvenirs, guns, cameras, medals, patches, wings, jump boots, knives, daggers. Anything with value. Jeez, you go off to fight one enemy and come back to another. And the guys were supposedly on our side.

I got settled in the winterized tent that would be my home and was going to do it then. But I received a three-day pass to Paris and left immediately, on February 28. When I returned, I couldn't put it off any longer. I wrote her.

March 3, 1945
France

Dear Faye,

Received your swell "V"-mail a couple of days ago and finally have found the time to answer. I had wanted to write you long ago but the government won't allow it until they are certain that enough time has elapsed.

I hardly know how to write this letter, Faye. Your loss has been so great that there is very little I can say that would in any way console you. He was my best friend and the hardest thing I've ever had to do was go on fighting after "the Skipper" was gone. I've seen a lot of them go, and I'd never seen men cry 'til that day when Skip joined the angels. Countless tears from a lot of his friends fell into the snow that day. He was without doubt the best liked person in the company—respected as a soldier—loved as the happy-go-lucky Skipper.

I've never missed Mass, Faye, and Sunday morning was always certain that I got out of the sack. That last Sunday [before Skip's death] we went to services in a snow-covered field in Belgium so we can be thankful in knowing that he was in the State of Grace.

I do hope and pray that someday I will be able to meet you. I've always felt as if I really did know you. If ever I do get back to New York I shall promise to come to Kenmore. I'd always planned to do that with Skip. I wanted to tell you how lucky I thought you were. Now I can only shudder at the anguish you must be enduring. Gosh! Faye, I wish I could spend several hours with you so I could tell you everything that I can't seem to put into words.

I hope you will write. I know he would have wanted it that way. "Chuck" [Grant] sends his regards. Joe [Toye] is in pretty

tough shape. "Smitty" [Burr Smith] is in the hospital, too, but
will be back soon.
   Love, Don

When Lieutenant Speirs offered me a ten-day furlough
in England, I grabbed it with gusto. Not only would it be
fun, but it would take my mind off other things, such as
Skip and the increasingly less enthusiastic letters from Bernice. "Never again say 'It's hard to keep our love alive when
we're so far apart,' " I wrote her in March. "It might be that
way for you but not for me. The only thing I find hard
about it is trying to quell the intensity of it enough to act
normal."

In England, I played lots of craps, sold a German
Schmeisser for $275 to some sailor while crossing the English
Channel, and ate frequently at a basement café on Charing
Cross Road that specialized in roast duck and browned potatoes. Marvelous. Somewhere along the line, I read that the
entire 101st Division had been awarded the Presidential Cita-
tion, the second time for the 506th, for its stance near Bastogne. Wearing that uniform with the screaming eagle on it,
people knew two things about you: You were a damn good
soldier—and half crazy.

One afternoon, in the basement bar of the Regent Palace
Hotel, I noticed two red-beret sergeants from the British 1st
Airborne Division sitting down the way. In London, these
guys were honored above all; nobody in a red beret was to
be arrested for drunkenness. Eventually they noticed my
101st Airborne patch, the screaming eagle.

"We owe a tip of the hat to the 101st," said one. "Got us
across the Rhine one black night after we'd been trapped
behind enemy lines."

I jiggled the ice cubes in my Scotch.

"I know," I said. "That was my company. E Company, 506th."

They scoffed a bit and looked around at each other, obviously thinking I was trying to take some credit that wasn't due me.

"Oh, *really?*" one said with a touch of doubt.

"Yeah," I said. "I was on the rescue team."

"Well, of course you were, old chap—so was my dead aunt Lucille," said one, and they both laughed.

My Scotch was settling in. I paused, then took another sip.

"Say, how's that tank sergeant, the commander from the Seventh Armored Division who headed up that outfit known as the Rats of Tobruk? Guy was in my boat."

Their eyes widened.

"After we got him safely across the Rhine, he told me his wife had already been a widow five times and he was gettin' out of this 'bloody war.' "

They froze in silence, then one of them cleared his throat. "To E Company," he said, holding up his drink. I clinked my glass with the others and nodded, then held mine high. "To E Company."

When I returned to Mourmelon, there was another letter from Faye. Among other things, she wondered why Skip's family hadn't gotten an official letter from the company, beyond the telegram. It probably got lost in the transition from Dike to Speirs, I figured. At any rate, Skip's mother was still holding out hope that her son was alive. I wrote back.

March 31, 1945
France

Dear Faye,

Just returned from a grand furlough in London and your swell letter was a real treat.

I'm sorry to hear you had been sick, Faye, but I'm sure that by this time you must be back to normal and enjoying yourself as much as possible in these days of war. Though I'll have to admit the way it's going now anything could happen. It's hard to believe that the Rhine is so far behind the line these days.

This damn war has been going so long that when it finally does end I won't be able to believe it.

I know how hard it is for you to realize Skip is gone. And how hard it must be to forget. I don't think things always happen for the best—they just happen and we have to try to adjust ourselves accordingly.

Perhaps we can console ourselves in that he is in a happier place where there is always peace and not the misery and horror of a crazy world at war.

I'm afraid that the telegram is official. The chaplain does write the family but it does take time. It's hell to think Skip's mother is still hoping. His personal things are also to be sent home by the chaplain. I'm sure that in time they will arrive.

Well, Faye, I'll close for now. I'm getting along great in spite of this G.D. life. You needn't worry about haunting me. I'll come to Kenmore. If anyone or anything ever does.

Love, Don

Allied forces were pushing deeper into Germany. On April 2, we were trucked to the west side of the Rhine River to act as blocking backs for any major escape attempts out of the Ruhr region. We were positioned in various villages, watching with interest as German citizens worked on their war-damaged properties rather than flee.

In a village named Dormagen, Lt. Harry Welsh was looking for someone to check on a factory on the Rhine where it was rumored German soldiers might be holed up. I said I'd go. I went out with a rifleman, Ralph Orth, about noon. We worked our way through the large building, finding nobody. On the way out, we were walking through the yard area. At times like this, you couldn't help thinking, after surviving all the tough stuff, if your number would come up on something simple like this. As I'd written Bernice, "I'm a fugitive from the law of averages, which isn't good."

"Hey, Orth," I asked. "How long's it been since you fired that rifle?"

"I dunno, Sarge. A long time, I guess."

I pointed to a stack of railroad rails about fifty yards away.

"Why don't you fire into that stack?"

He aimed and fired, then immediately yelled, "I'm hit!" and crumbled to the ground. What the hell? At first I thought he was joking, then we realized he'd been hit by a fragment of his own bullet that had hit a steel rail and ricocheted. It had penetrated his kneecap.

"Thanks, Sarge," he said, his look of fear suddenly replaced by a smile. "You just earned me a ticket home."

Our life now was not day-to-day combat, but mop-up duty. Patrols here and there to check for enemy soldiers holed up in various places. "Remember this," Speirs once told us. "No prisoners. Shoot 'em all."

One night, we crossed the Rhine to check for krauts in some building and, finding none, were returning when machine-gun fire hailed down on us. We were still about fifty feet from the shore. It was a mad rush for the bank but none of us got hit.

In some ways, as the strength of the real enemy diminished, another enemy rose up: ourselves. Sometimes it was serious, some guy getting drunk and killing another guy, other times just some alcohol-fueled high jinks, like the night I showed up at the company headquarters soaking wet from having jumped into the Rhine in the middle of the night, fueled by the strangest booze I've ever had.

They told me it was schnapps. It turned out to be wood alcohol, probably 200 proof, and it locked up my respiratory system like a frozen block on a pickup. I couldn't breathe. I started flailing my arms in anguish, which only heightened the laughter from the guys around me. But Floyd Talbert realized I was in trouble. He threw me down on a cot and jumped on my chest. My breathing started again. Once recovered, I picked up a bottle of the stuff, poured it in an ashtray, and dropped a match in it. The flames leapt into the air like a homecoming bonfire.

Several nights later, I was lying in my bunk and broke out into a deep sweat, followed by chills. Back and forth. Finally, our medic, Eugene Roe, came and took my temperature.

"We're gettin' you the hell out of here, Malark."

"No, no, no. I'll be OK."

Nobody in Easy had spent more consecutive days in combat than me. I didn't want the streak to end because I had a piddly case of the flu.

"I'm getting Speirs," said Roe.

"Roe, I'm—"

"Shut up, Malark. You're sick."

He got Captain Speirs, who did a quick assessment and

ordered me to a hospital. "We're pulling out in the morning, Malark. You're not fit to come. Get well and rejoin us for the victory celebration in Hitler's place in the mountains."

An ambulance took me to a field hospital, where I hazily recall several doctors standing over me, bright lights in my face, and hearing talk about some strain of Rhine River malaria.

The next day, I was sent to an army hospital at the University of Liège in Belgium. It was there, in Liège, that the German drive to Antwerp had stalled. I was assigned a bed abutting a windowed outside wall, directly across from a platoon sergeant from the 28th Division. The guy had been here since the Bulge, when he'd frozen his feet off in the Ardennes Forest, and was in serious pain. Fourteen beds lined each side of the room.

In the days to come, I made the weirdest discovery: Except for the sarge across from me, nobody there was really sick. And the doctors and nurses seemed to be playing right along with the script. The patients would kid around like guys on some fraternity porch, then someone would whistle, and everyone would hop back in his bed. As the door opened, they'd paste these poor-me looks on their faces. In would walk some major from the medical staff, going from bed to bed, listening to the wildest stories of woe imaginable. And with apparent sympathy. What kind of Mickey Mouse outfit was this?

Finally, the doctor reached my bed, looked at my chart, and asked how I felt.

"Fine," I said. "Whatever I had must have broken in the time I was being shuttled here from the Rhine."

"According to this chart, Sergeant Malarkey, what you have is more serious than you might think."

I shrugged. "All I can tell you is I feel fine. I'd like to get back to my company." He looked at me with furrowed brow and moved on. This went on for days—the well people acting sick and me telling the major that I was well and ready to get out of this place.

"Sergeant, why do you want out of here?"

I couldn't stand it anymore. "Because someone's gotta fight the friggin' war!" I said.

Just when I didn't think his brow could furrow any further, it did. "Are you—are you *serious?*"

"Damn right I'm serious."

Guy thought I was nuts. "You *want* back out there?"

This went on for ten days. It was as if I were trapped in some freakish theater comedy. But it would have been funnier had it not been sickening; these were a bunch of yellow-bellied cowards turning their backs on the country they'd promised to serve.

Next day, I was told the doctor wanted me on an upper-floor lab. He wanted to give me something called sodium pentothal, as part of an examination.

"What the hell is that stuff?" I asked.

"It's a drug that'll relax you and help you describe your feelings."

I wanted to tell him that I was quite capable of describing my feelings without his shooting me full of that crap. Like this: *I feel like I'd like to punch you in your furrowed-brow face and leave this loony bin forever.*

He offered me an afternoon pass into Liège. "Walk around, get some fresh air, Sergeant Malarkey, and let's see how you get along," he said.

I thought about just bolting, but figured going AWOL this late in the game wasn't a good idea. I got along just fine and returned, ready to pack and leave.

"Wait, wouldn't you want to donate some blood for us?" the doctor said. "We could use a pint."

"You can get all the blood you need from these crybabies around me," I said.

And I left, knowing that the guys in Easy would never believe this one. When I walked out of that hospital, I felt freer than I had felt since the night I'd sat around that campfire on the Nehalem River before leaving for the army.

When the war in Europe ended, I was in a pub in Verviers, Belgium. All by myself. Trying to figure out how in the hell I was going to find my division. I had come to Verviers because I knew that an army transient facility there helped soldiers get reconnected to their units.

After Bastogne, the Belgians would see that eagle on my shoulder and buy me drinks on the spot, so I was enjoying some of that hospitality in a sidewalk pub on the town's main street when it happened: Out of nowhere, the church bells started ringing. Then I heard some shouts.

"It's over!" people started yelling in all sorts of languages, including some in broken English. "The war is over! The Germans have surrendered!"

I hoisted my mug in the air. Others did the same. This was a country the Germans had goose-stepped into in 1940 and basically said, *You are now under our rule.* Except for a few months after the original Allied sweep toward Germany, they hadn't known freedom for nearly twice the time I'd been in the service. They'd lost sons in battle. Lost civilians who got caught in the cross fire of war. People were hugging each other. Kissing each other. Dancing.

Belgians. Americans. Brits. Canadians. All wrapped together in a sort of frenzied celebration born of pain and loss and a million memories we all wanted to forget but knew we never would.

Only one thing was missing: Easy Company. My band of brothers. As much fun as I was having with the locals, it wasn't quite the same without a connection to those guys whom I'd been with since Toccoa. You could look in those guys' eyes and, without saying a word, feel a connection I'd never felt before or would ever feel again. As if our strength hadn't come from being Don, Skip, Joe, Bill, Frank, Burr, Gordon, and the rest, but from being one single unit. Not perfect; hell, far from it. But absolutely committed to one another amid our imperfection. And to doing whatever it took to win this war.

Shortly after, as if I'd had a prayer answered, I looked through the window and saw him: Frank Perconte, a 1st Platooner in Easy Company, a good-looking Italian from Chicago. I'd last seen him in the snow of Bastogne, bleeding badly from the neck, not thinking he was going to make it.

"Malark!"

"Perconte, you old son of a—"

"Let me buy you a drink, or a dozen!"

"I wasn't sure you'd even made it," I said. "You OK?"

"Just a scratch."

Turns out he was headed back to rejoin the company after recovering in England. Somehow, just having one Easy Company guy there made all the difference. And the day only got better when a trolley rolled up out front and there, perched on top, was someone familiar to us both: Burr Smith. He, too, was returning after a wound at Bastogne.

The three of us locked arms around each other.

"This is it, boys," said Smith. "We're going home!"

15
DREAMING OF WILD BLACKBERRIES

Germany, Austria
May 9, 1945–Mid-June 1945

Home was never quite as close as we'd think. After we'd caught up with Easy Company in Saalfelden, Austria, in mid-May, all of us were packing our bags and heading for the nearest ship back to the States—at least in our minds. But then you'd start hearing the name of a place that none of us had given much thought to.

Japan. War in Europe was over, yes, but many in the 101st might be shipped to the Pacific. There was talk of an invasion of the Japanese mainland. Your future depended on your "points," which were based on months of active duty, campaigns, medals, and whether you were married. I was five or ten short from a ticket home. Where was Bernice when I needed her?

I'd written her in May, when hearing that those going to

the Pacific would get twenty-one days of leave in the States before shipping out. "For twenty-one glorious days we'll make up for the almost three years of heartache and loneliness," I wrote. I wanted to marry her as soon as possible. "Perhaps," I wrote, "it would be wiser to wait till the war is over and I have some sort of a decent job, but I don't know if it pays to be wise."

By the time Perconte, and Smith, and I rejoined the guys, the division had captured Hitler's famed Eagle's Nest at Berchtesgaden, Germany. Yeah, we'd missed that fun, including Hitler's private wine cellar, but plenty of good times were still to be had.

After Saalfelden, we moved on to Kaprun, Austria, where we were housed in knotty-pine duplexes, formerly occupied by German engineers. The city of Zell am See, between Kaprun and Saalfelden, was a jewel nestled in the Alps. There, we swam, boated, and simply soaked in the kind of warmth that, in Bastogne, I'd forgotten existed.

We were no longer a combat outfit but an occupation force. To the winner goes the spoils—so goes the saying, and so went Easy Company. First to reach Hitler's much ballyhooed Eagle's Nest perch high in the Alps, my buddies had cashed in big-time with souvenirs, and also ransacked the personal train of Hermann Göring, the Nazi's second-in-command. Most of the good stuff was gone by the time I arrived, but I still found ways to get some wonderful mementos.

Few were more ambitious with souvenirs than Alton More, the guy who'd somehow found a way to get that motorcycle and sidecar on the LST back in Normandy. He had come out of the Eagle's Nest with two of Hitler's picture albums showing him meeting with foreign delegations. One of the privates in the platoon came after me one day, telling me of a confrontation between More and a company officer who was demanding the albums. Alton threatened the officer, who in turn threatened a court-martial. I went to Winters at Battalion to defend More.

Winters listened, then said, "Come with me, Don." He took me down to his jeep driver and said to him, "Take Sergeant Malarkey back to his quarters and return with Private More and all his gear." Somehow, this didn't seem right; More hadn't done anything wrong. But Winters, as always, was one step ahead of us. He made More his personal jeep driver, a sort of shot across the bow to the company officer.

More was always thinking. After his new assignment, he took the jeep to Saalfelden, where he had a shoemaker turn one of the seat cushions into a carrying case for his albums. He carried it with him at all times.

Meanwhile, Don Moone, in the interest of being well fed, became a waiter in the officers' mess. And, more important, kept his ears wide-open when he was serving the brass so he could pick up all the latest information on what Easy Company's future held. Moone heard that if you were going to Japan, you'd get a thirty-day furlough in the States, then would have to report back for duty.

Not me. I'd all but made up my mind. If that was the case, I was going to go home, period. If the army wanted me in Japan, they'd have to come get me. And I wouldn't tell them which bend in the Nehalem River I'd be fishing. I'd seen enough war. Not to brag, but when I got sent to that hospital in Liège, it ended the longest streak of consecutive days of combat of anyone in the company, 177 days. I'd given enough, seen enough, and left my best friend buried back in Belgium, in pieces. I was through with war. I wanted to go home and marry Bernice. But I wasn't sure she wanted to marry me.

In late May, Moone overheard a conversation between a second lieutenant and Captain Speirs.

"You should bust Malarkey," said the lieutenant.

"And why should I do that?" asked Speirs.

"Because guys in his outfit are fraternizing with Austrian girls."

"Well, I'm not busting Sergeant Malarkey," Speirs said. "He'll go to Japan with us—but I'm not so sure about you."

Moone was always hearing this tip or that. Once, he asked if I had any teeth that needed filling and took me to the house of a Dr. Franz Pasler, an Austrian dentist who worked on my teeth as Moone visited with his wife. As we were leaving, I noticed a number of photographs of a young athlete, both in ski and track attire. It was the couple's son, who had been a member of the Austrian Olympics team in both sports for the 1936 Olympics.

On a return visit—the doctor's wife was making us some good deals on jewelry she was getting from her husband's cousin in Vienna—we heard a noise upstairs. When we pressed them about who it was, she broke down and admitted it was her son, who had been forced into the German army, had become an officer, but fled.

"Please," she said. "My son will not hurt anyone."

The deeper we'd gotten into war, and into Germany, the more we'd realized that their soldiers weren't much different than ours. I was serving my country when asked; they were only doing the same.

I looked at Moone. He looked at me. We moved to the hallway to talk in private, then returned to where Mrs. Pasler was standing.

"Son?" I said. "What son?" And we left, never regretting not reporting him.

Over, yes. But that didn't mean all was bliss. Guys who'd survived a year of war were getting killed in car wrecks. Starting to lose their edge of discipline. James Alley and a bunch of others got busted for being drunk.

One night, some replacement guy in our company got liquored up and killed a couple of German soldiers at a patrol spot on a road. The 2nd Platoon fanned out to find this guy, who was loose, drunk, and brandishing a gun. Sgt. Chuck Grant flushed him out of a building and brought his arm up under the guy's hand to dislodge his gun. It went off, the bullet going through Grant's head. Blood streamed down his face, around his ear, and down his neck.

Grant was still alive, but barely. We got Chuck to the hospital and the German doctor who examined him said it was useless; he'd die from the shock of the operation. At that point, Hank "Hack" Hansen went berserk, pulling a gun on the doc. Hansen was Grant's best friend.

"Save him or I'll kill you!" he said, jamming the gun to the guy's head. "Save him!"

The doctor reconsidered. He came out hours later and said the patient was still alive. The doctor was amazed. "Toughest man I've ever seen," he told us in broken English.

Our manners toward the doctor improved after Chuck recovered. In fact, in June, Captain Speirs organized a company banquet at a low-level ski lodge to honor the man for saving Chuck's life. I wound up sitting next to the doctor. He told me he'd never seen anyone so far gone survive. During the dinner, he leaned over to me and in broken English said, "By the way, do you think that man would have shot me?"

I didn't hesitate in my response. "Yes." I nodded. "I think he would have. I really do."

The man looked and me and nodded his head slightly. "Please thank him for pulling the gun on me."

One day a few of us took a ski lift to the top of a mountain. Six months earlier, I'd been curled up in a ball in a frozen foxhole in the darkness of a forest, trying to come to terms with the death of my best friend. Now, I was looking out at a vista like none other I'd ever seen, white-capped peaks stretching forever, sharply contrasting with a sky that couldn't have been painted any bluer. It was summer. A slight breeze cooled us. Looking east, you could see Germany and imagine where we'd been: Belgium, Holland, England, France. Even imagine where we *might* be: across that giant puddle between here and America, where I'd be going to see two special women—my girl, Bernice, and Skip's girl, Faye—then on to Oregon. I wanted to marry Bernice, then get into some sort of foreign-trade business, thinking that would be a good future because of America's new, and hard-earned, power in the world.

But I continued to have doubts about my future with Bernice. On June 6, the one-year anniversary of D-day, I wrote to Bernice and suggested that perhaps she'd "outgrown" me. She was aspiring to be a famous singer. "I'm still and always will be an ordinary sort of guy. Because of that, I'm now skeptical as to whether we'll get married. The smartest thing you could do would be to grab some rich young bachelor. It's going to be a long, hard road with me, darling, I know it.

I really don't have any right to ask you to marry me. All I have to offer you is love. . . ."

In previous letters, she'd encouraged me to write a book about my war experiences. "You flattered me so much I'm bewildered," I wrote, "[but] right now I'm not capable of writing anything. I have been deeply hurt and the wounds won't heal for awhile." I was referring to my status within Easy Company, how someone had tried to get me busted out. How everything had changed since I'd gone into the hospital. Some new leadership. Some new fears. At one point, I was so angry and frustrated with how I was being treated that I offered to turn in my stripes, but my superior wouldn't accept them.

Truth be told, I was also deeply hurt by Bernice. Her letters were fewer and farther in between. "I don't know whether I should keep writing you or not," I wrote. "I'd hate to experience what my friend R.B. ["Burr"] Smith did. He wrote his girl, almost daily, for three months. Letters that were dripping with love and enduring promises. He hadn't heard from her for some time and credited the lapse to the fact that he had been hospitalized for awhile and as a result his mail delayed. In the end one of his friends finally told him what the story was. She was married."

On that same June day that I'd written Bernice, we in Easy Company celebrated the one-year anniversary since our drop into Normandy that began what, without doubt, would be the most adventurous, uplifting, and anguishing year of our lives.

Easy Company was about to break up. The 506th was being inactivated; those from the 101st would be redeployed to the Pacific after a winter furlough back home. Meanwhile, General Taylor—the guy not smart enough to figure out that any live soldier wearing a helmet with a chunk of it missing must have been wearing it at the time he was hit— ordered the division to begin a full training regime. Our hearts weren't in it.

At Kaprun, Easy Company lined up for a final photo, the 506th flag being waved in the middle, me way off to the left. Soon after the photo session, Winters called me to battalion.

"Don," he said, "you've been selected by the division to be technical adviser to an Airborne display in a very nice place. It's called Paris. In fact, right beneath the Eiffel Tower. You'll be on detached service to the air force."

Sounded a helluva lot better than Japan. I reached out to shake his hand, my eyes locked on his, knowing what he was really telling me was that I'd given enough. And this was my reward.

"Thank you, sir, for everything."

"I'll personally take you to the airport in Salzburg tomorrow."

I saluted him. Instead of saluting back, he extended a hand to shake.

The next day I was picked up by Winters in a command car. On the way, we stopped at Division supply for fuel. While we waited, Dick spotted someone.

"Watch who comes out," he said.

In a moment, there was Sobel, who was now a supply officer for the regiment. Sobel noticed me first, not Winters. He looked at me with furrowed brow.

"You Malarkey?" he said.

I nodded as he looked at my uniform. He'd left me as a private; I was now a platoon sergeant. "Hmmm," he said. "Looks like you've done some things since I last saw you."

Until then, our last interaction, by letter, had been regarding a motorcycle and sidecar taken from Normandy.

Winters cleared his throat. "Don't you salute a superior officer?"

Sobel realized who it was and froze.

"You're not saluting the man, you're saluting the rank," said Winters.

Sobel whipped the fastest salute I'd ever seen. With the war over, I found myself with a kind of odd respect for Herbert Sobel. I didn't like him, but I didn't hate him either. Sometimes, the people we've struggled with can help us get through the toughest times of our lives.

My father quit. I vowed I wouldn't. Then I was flung into this thing called war, where the whole idea is just that: Make the other guy give up. You throw shells and mortars and grenades and bullets at him. You mix in the elements: rain, fog, mud, snow, ice, and cold like you've never known them. Then you add the stuff they don't talk much about in war, the stuff that got to a guy like Buck Compton: the heartache of two buddies, legs blown apart, helpless in the snow. Suddenly you're standing around that fire in Bastogne, thinking of putting a bullet through your leg. Then your best friend is killed, and you want to curl up and die. *Quit.*

But somewhere, deep down, you hear that voice as you're running up Currahee: "The men of Easy Company do not quit! Do you *understand* me?" And so you don't. If anything, that's the legacy of Easy Company. Not that we were bigger, stronger, faster, or more skilled. But that we didn't give in when it hurt, didn't give up when we wanted to. Didn't quit.

Sobel's inspiration was hidden so deeply in us—and obscured so badly by his pain-in-the-ass style—that most of us may not even have noticed it. But despite his cruelty, he did manage to develop in us an esprit de corps that's never left us, a bond born of going through hell for the SOB. Winters, the man now driving me away from this war, was the best damn leader I've ever known, though it took me decades to tell him that. Those two men, and the bonds with every man around us, made the "band of brothers" what we were.

Winters nodded at Sobel, the two exchanging a hint of respect, then pulled away. I rolled down my window, leaned my head back, and, smiling, imagined the smell of late-summer blackberries in Oregon.

16

THE WAR THAT NEVER ENDS

New York, Oregon
November 29, 1945–Present

Officially, I parted ways with Uncle Sam on November 29, 1945, at Fort Dix in New Jersey. I was given my back pay, my craps earnings, and asked if I had claims to make against the U.S. government. No, our slates were clean; they'd thrown me together with the greatest group of men imaginable. I'd helped them win a war. In return, I got a certificate of appreciation. "Proud to help out," I told the guy who stamped my discharge papers. With a few signatures, the army was suddenly behind me.

Thanks, of course, to an atomic bomb. After it was dropped in August, more than three months before my discharge, the Japanese had surrendered. After about six years—nearly four of U.S. involvement—World War II was over. By now, soldiers were flooding back home and I was damn glad to be one of them.

I wanted to see two people in New York upon my return, but after lots of wrangling in my mind, I realized I had the guts to see only one: Bernice. She and her mother came to see me at Fort Dix, shortly before I was discharged. It was a happy reunion, though, as always with Bernice and me, tinged with uncertainty.

I checked in to the Henry Hudson Hotel. I fell asleep in America for the first time in more than three years as a civilian again. The Hudson was no Astor Hotel, but you spend enough nights in a foxhole or a henhouse and anything that's soft, roomy, and doesn't smell like chicken manure makes you feel like a king. I slept well.

In the days and nights to come, Bernice and I did a bunch of fast-paced catching up: her singing with the Phil Spitalny All-Girl Orchestra; my time in postwar Paris. Her practice schedule; my plans to fly back home. Her family; my family, or what was left of it, given Grandma Malarkey's death and my father's continuing funk.

Bernice and I spent three days together. Going to clubs. Running errands, including getting my craps money in a bank. Talking about the future. Our future.

"Why don't we look at engagement rings?" I asked.

She hesitated. "There's plenty of time for that, Don. Why don't we wait a bit, let you get back home and get unpacked."

I agreed. Meanwhile, I realized that with Bernice busy with singing practice and performances, I could make a quick trip north to Kenmore, New York, and keep my promise to Faye. We'd talked about it in letters we'd exchanged since Skip's death. Yes, I needed to do that. But when I arrived at Grand Central Station, I couldn't get on that train. Looking back, it'd be funny if it weren't so sad. I'd just survived World War II, but I couldn't go to my dead friend's fiancée like I'd promised her I would.

It wasn't that I was afraid of all the emotions that my visit would unleash, what with both of us thinking the world of a guy who was now just a picture on her mantel. And it wasn't that I didn't *want* to see her; hell, I wanted to see her in the worst way.

That was the problem. After listening to Skip talk about Faye for a couple of years and after writing her back and forth after his death, I felt that I knew her almost as well as I knew Bernice. Plus, in some strange way, I suppose I thought being with her would somehow bring a little bit of Skip back. To be blunt, what kept me from going to see Faye Tanner was that I was convinced that if I met her, I'd fall in love with her right on the spot.

And I couldn't do that to Skip. It wouldn't be fair to take a guy's girl when he wasn't even around to fight back, especially when that guy was the best friend you'd ever had.

On my last day in New York, I dressed in the only clothes I had—the 101st eagle stitched on the shoulder of my jacket—and got on the hotel elevator, along with some upper-floor tenants. Across the elevator stood a distinguished-looking man, a mink muffler wrapped around his neck, holding a jeweled umbrella and wearing a homburg. After looking at me, he quickly removed his hat.

"Sergeant," he said. "I salute you." And did so.

He looked vaguely familiar but I couldn't place him. I just

nodded a thanks, feeling a bit embarrassed. He got off on the next floor.

"You must be something special," said the woman next to me. "I ride the elevator with him every day and he's never removed his hat for anyone."

"Who in the hel—uh, who is he?" I asked.

"That is the premier tenor of the New York Metropolitan Opera, Mr. Lauritz Melchior."

Nobody asked who I was, which is just as well. After being saluted by one of the finest voices in the world, my buttons were about to pop. Only later would I learn why seeing my 101st Airborne patch had meant so much to him. I'd forgotten: Melchior was Danish. The Germans had occupied his homeland for five years.

Incidents like that made a guy feel good. I remember another one involving another famous person, General Patton. The previous July, two months after V-E Day, along with some other Easy Company guys, I was on a three-day pass and wound up in the "U" section of one of Hitler's stadiums in a city named Worms. In the morning, the head of the facility came to me, the ranking noncom, and asked us to come salute Patton, who was coming by for an inspection. At the appointed hour, we heard sirens. Motorcycles led Patton's staff car in, flags flying. His car stopped. I called our group to attention.

Patton looked us over and said something about the 101st Airborne Division I'll never forget: "If I had two divisions of you bastards, I would have had the Germans blowing straws up their asses by Thanksgiving and you would have been home by Christmas."

Maybe so. Instead, we'd fought nearly six more months of war, which, in retrospect, had soured Bernice on any future we might have. She had a career to launch. I had a war to fight. The two proved to be giant obstacles. In New York that day, I kissed her good-bye—she couldn't believe that *the* Lauritz Melchior had paid me such respect—with the understanding that I'd be back. But I think we both wondered if that would really happen.

Airlines were booked for weeks. Soldiers were trying to get home. It was Christmastime. I took a train. In Portland, I was met at the station by my aunts and uncles and cousins. A cousin, Hugh, ran at me full tilt, eyes full of tears, catching me by surprise.

"I thought you'd never get home, Donnie!" he said, then wrapped me in a bear hug.

The reception at home was warm with my mother and sister, but, as usual, awkward with my father. Not quite like that famous *Saturday Evening Post* cover where everybody stops what they're doing to notice a soldier's return. My father didn't have any emotions anymore that amounted to a hill of beans. He shook my hand as if he hardly knew me.

A light rain was falling. I grabbed an umbrella and went to see Gram's grave in the Ocean View Cemetery. Looking at the two headstones next to hers, Gerald's and Bob's, I couldn't help thinking she was finally back with the two boys she'd lost to war. I stood there in that cemetery with all sorts of mixed feelings, remembering the words of my grandmother: *If anything happens to you, Donnie Malarkey, it'll be the end of me.* She'd gone to bed on D-day and never gotten up. A wonderful woman, the closest thing to a saint I'd ever know. But I hope she died knowing I'd kept my end of the bargain. I'd stayed alive. And though nobody gave a hoot about it but me, in a strange way I'd also kept my deal with my uncles, who I somehow imagined being proud of me. I'd brought home a P38 pistol, not a Luger. It didn't matter. *We, the Malarkey boys, we made it.*

Above, a squadron of seagulls flew by. In the distance, the Pacific Ocean crashed ashore, and smelling the salt air, I was reminded how much I loved the wildness of this state. The last beach I'd seen, Utah Beach, was strewn with the litter of war. I'm not one of these guys who prays all the time, but in war I'd prayed lots. And in that cemetery, I thanked God for the answers, even if they weren't all quite what I'd wanted.

Later, at the Liberty Grill, I scarfed down a hamburger steak and mashed potatoes, catching up with Bernice's folks between bites. It's not like heads turned whenever someone in Astoria saw Don Malarkey home from the war, but I'd been the only paratrooper from Clatsop County. They'd read about the Screaming Eagles. And so it wasn't surprising to have someone buy me a meal now and then.

After dinner, I drove to the top of the hill that Astoria is chiseled into, above the old house on Kensington, and looked west, to the mouth of the Columbia River where it empties into the Pacific. I thought of Bernice, how she could be standing in a building in New York and look east and see the harbor that empties into the Atlantic. It reminded me how much distance there was between us. If we were to marry, would she—a New York City singer who wanted to sing internationally—be happy back here in Oregon, where even Portland, the state's largest city, was backwoods in the eyes of the Big Apple? And what about me? What do you get in New York City to replace the Nehalem River? Or the simplicity of Eugene, where I could literally walk two blocks from the frat and be on campus, another six and be downtown watching a flick at the McDonald Theatre? Somehow, I was afraid that distance between us was just too much.

I stayed in the Cow Creek cabin for a few weeks. Took lots of walks along the Nehalem, the river swollen from Oregon's infamous winter rains, the blackberries still six months away, and left the day after Christmas for the University of Oregon. Just like I'd promised Ike when he'd shaken my hand in England while reviewing the troops, I was going back to school.

Despite three years in the service—I was now twenty-four—I got back in the swing of college; it wasn't as if there weren't a few other GIs in their midtwenties doing the same thing. But every now and then I was reminded that everything wasn't the same. *I* wasn't the same.

Sure, I still had the zest for fun. Still loved to sing the big-band songs. Still liked an occasional drink. But I'd been to war. And coming home, you can't just check it at the door like a hat or a coat. I'd see or hear things that would suddenly bring it all back: a combat movie at the McDonald. The eyes of some freshman who reminded me of that sixteen-year-old German kid I'd shot in Foy. The backfire of a truck; once, on Thirteenth Street, that happened and I literally dove for cover because it was still so ingrained in me.

Every now and then, I'd wake up tangled in my blankets and sweating like a pig, sure some German soldier had just popped out from behind those skinny firs in Jack's Woods and jammed a bayonet in my gut. Or those bloody legs of Toye's and Guarnere's in the snow. But would you tell anyone about this stuff back then? Hell, no, even though, when you're sleeping in a fraternity sleeping porch, it's hard to hide thrashing around like that.

I'd served thirty days of combat in Normandy, seventy-eight in Holland, thirty-nine in Bastogne, and thirty in Haguenau. And I wonder if, with war becoming such a part of you, you become like the Toyes and Guarneres of the world, people who lose a limb and yet have that phantom sensation that it's still there.

Sometimes, I couldn't get back to sleep. Or I'd just read or try studying at a desk, not that I was very good at that. I couldn't concentrate like before the war. I'd be reading some book and suddenly realize Roe was sitting beside me. *Malark, I'm sorry, but it's Skip . . .* I feared my grades were slipping badly.

Once, a guy in the house who'd been in the navy started asking me all these questions about what it was like to jump out of a plane with a parachute, and before you knew it, he had me up on top of my desk, demonstrating. I was going through the whole works, you know, when I heard some snickering behind me; there, in the hallway, were a bunch of frat brothers watching, laughing like hell. It had been a setup, a joke just to make me look like a fool. At the time, I wasn't laughing.

I remembered after Skip had died and how I'd wanted to write to Faye but the government wouldn't allow it. I was told I couldn't write her until they were certain "enough time has elapsed." Just how much time is "enough?" Outside, I was Joe College. Inside, I was still Sgt. Don Malarkey.

One day, I took out a photo of Easy Company and a black felt pen. Starting in the front row, left to right, and going upward in rows, I looked at every man in that photograph—117. For some reason, I marked "KIA" on the chests of those who'd been killed in action and "SWA" on the chests of those who'd been seriously wounded in action. There were thirty-five KIAs. And sixty-one SWAs. That left fewer than two dozen of us with clean chests. And, for that matter, clean consciences because of survivor's guilt. Which is why I'd look at that picture and feel the tears coming on nearly every time.

In March, I had a call from Bernice. She was in Astoria, visiting her folks, who liked the idea of their daughter maybe marrying a hometown boy. I agreed to take a bus to see her. Her mother was cordial to me, but her dad was cool to me, as if he knew a wedding between me and his daughter wasn't to be. We all ate at the Liberty Grill, and then Bernice and I drove her family's Pontiac upriver, to a hill overlooking Tongue Point, where plenty of neckers were fogging up the windows. We'd been up there plenty of times, but tonight it was different. We looked out at the navy ships anchored on the Columbia below. There was lots of awkward silence.

"Bernice," I finally blurted out, "I'm too damn mixed up to even think about getting married, much less going to New York."

She understood. In some ways, I think she was relieved. We parted friends, this time for good. I thanked her for all the letters that had been morale boosters for me during the war. "You helped me keep my sanity," I said. "Or at least part of it." I returned to Eugene, for whatever was in store for me there, and Bernice returned to New York and her first love, her singing career.

Come summer, I moved to Portland to work at Monarch Forge and Machine Works, where I'd worked before the war.

Where that German soldier I'd met in Normandy had worked across the street. I remember thinking, *Whatever happened to him? Where is he now?* (Unlike in the HBO *Band of Brothers* miniseries, he and the other prisoners we'd encountered had not been gunned down by Captain Speirs right after that; I'd like to think the soldier was shipped to a POW camp in America, released after the war, and is now enjoying his grandchildren's soccer games in Munich.)

While in Portland, I lived with my mom's parents, Grandma and Granddad Trask. It was a pretty hard time for me, living away from my pals, struggling at school, breaking it off with Bernice. I remember that Sinatra song "I'll Never Smile Again," playing over and over, as if to remind me.

A few weeks later a car pulled up in front of the house. It was John Warren, our fraternity's adviser, a guy who had coached many of Astoria's great basketball players and come to the University of Oregon to be an assistant basketball coach. I respected him highly.

"Don," he said, "I've got some bad news. You're flunking out. You and 460 others, mostly vets."

I didn't know what to say. Other than my ROTC washout, I'd not failed at much in my life.

"Hey," he said, "I know it can't be easy, with the war and all, Donnie, but it's sink-or-swim time, pal. I've pulled some strings. Got you a meeting with George Hall, assistant dean of men. See if we can get you back in school. Will you do it?"

I felt pretty small about then. Hell, I could go out on night patrol in Holland, take eight guys prisoner, but now I couldn't get a passing grade in political science. At first I thought, *What's the use?* Then I thought again.

Warren was a little like Dick Winters, one of those guys

who believed in you and made you want to bust your butt for him. "Sure, John, I'll meet with him."

Hall was putting his neck on the line for me; he said he'd vouch for me, scholastically, if I wanted to file an appeal to get back in. I did. Two weeks later, he called. Six of the 460 had been reinstated. I was among them. I quit my job in Portland and moved back to Eugene to take a few summer courses.

One night, in early November, I was returning to the Sigma Nu house after completing an assignment in the library—not the kind of thing I would have done the previous term—when I stopped at the College Side Inn for a Coke. It was to become the most momentous soft drink I'd ever had. The inn was an English-style gathering spot with candy and soft drinks. The interior was all-natural dark wood with counters, booths, balconies, and a large meeting room.

She was with some other Gamma Phi Beta sorority sisters in a booth near the front: blond hair. A great smile. And brown eyes that made you want to look into them forever. I was smitten from the get-go with this gal. Her name was Irene Moor.

"Will you join us, Don?" someone asked.

They didn't need to ask me twice. I sat next to Irene and enjoyed getting to know her a little. She was from Portland, a Gamma Phi pledge. Later, when she brushed past me to get out of the booth, I thought a bolt of lightning had struck me. It was like nothing I'd ever experienced in my life—OK, *once,* when Bernice had brushed past me when we were high school freshmen. But this was different. I hadn't been back at the Sigma Nu house more than an hour when, through a friend who knew her, I'd arranged a date.

We started seeing each other a lot. I remember singing some Sinatra songs to her in the Pioneer Cemetery across from McArthur Court, a gesture that she loved and which apparently made up for my being a klutz when it came to jitterbug dancing.

Meanwhile, my grades started improving. The Sigma Nus started reestablishing themselves in the classroom, the intramural ball fields, and, of course, the social scene. I cheered on the University of Oregon's sports teams. Tipped more than a few in their honor. Became president of the fraternity. Took a fraternity house known for being jocks and whipped them into good enough shape as singers to win the all-campus sing. My frat brothers started calling me Little Caesar and Sarge for my demanding leadership style.

I landed a job at the Spudnut Doughnut Shop on Eleventh Street, across from the frat. I'd be at work at 5:30 A.M., do my job, head off for school, do my homework in the evening, and hit the sleeping porch at midnight. The nightmares started to fade. Not go away altogether. Just fade.

At the same time, doubts about whether I was worthy of Irene Moor started to tease me. I'd gone to Portland to meet her parents. She lived in a pretty classy neighborhood. Her father was an optician. Country-club types. And I was Don Malarkey, a guy who'd worked the salmon nets, spent a few years in foxholes, and now worked at a Spudnut Doughnut. I'm not sure her parents found me inspiring.

But one thing I knew and they knew: I loved their daughter. And one of the biggest reasons was because she was different from anybody else when it came to my war stuff. She listened. She understood. When all the sudden I'd be in tears over some stupid thing, she wouldn't think I was some sort of wimp. I told her stuff about the war, stuff that I'd never told anyone in the fraternity. During the war, she'd been to a lot of bases, being part of social events to keep up morale. She understood soldiers. And though she didn't understand war, she always gave me the benefit of the doubt, figuring that I'd seen stuff that was hard letting go of, even if I wanted to.

In the late spring, at midnight, following sorority closing hours, a choral group from the Chi Psi fraternity was serenading the Gamma Phis. When members appeared at the second-floor balcony, the group requested to see Miss Irene Moor. She was informed that she had been chosen "Moonlight Girl of Chi Psi Fraternity." But their voices wouldn't do much to win her over. She was mine. That was my Sigma Nu pin on her, shining in the moonlight, and when they realized it, their notes took a decided shift to the flat side.

I spent Easter weekend with her and her parents in Portland. I had brought her an Easter basket and positioned in a large decorative egg was an engagement ring.

"One thing you should know," I said. "You marry me, you marry me forever. No divorcing. I'm Catholic."

She had been raised Methodist. "But what if you don't love me any longer?" she asked.

"You won't have to worry about me never loving you any longer," I said.

We walked on. "One other thing," I said.

"Yes?"

"We should have a son and call him Michael."

"Why Michael?"

"I just like the sound of it: *Michael Malarkey.* Like the way it rolls off the tongue. Good Irish name."

"Michael Malarkey," she said. "You're right. Fine by me."

We were married June 19, 1948, the same day the rest of

my class was going through the graduation ceremony at the University of Oregon. I had earned my degree and could have been there, too, but I had a more important ceremony to attend.

We did have a son named Michael, who wound up serving with the 3rd Armored Division in Germany during the early seventies. And three wonderful daughters. I ran for county commissioner of Clatsop County, my old home county, and won. I sold cars at Lovell Auto in Astoria for years; once had a guy come up to me and shake my hand. It was Ben Gronnell.

"Son, I've been waiting fifteen years to say thank you to you," he said. "When you were just a little kid, you helped save my farm in the Tillamook Burn." I was, to say the least, surprised. He had tears in his eyes.

You start looking back over your life and realize that, for better or worse, the past never really goes away. It's with us always. Sometimes, like in the case of Ben Gronnell, it comes back to remind us maybe we're not so bad after all. And sometimes it comes back to haunt us; once, I went to my folks to get those German stamp books that I'd sent home. They didn't have them. Along with all the letters I'd sent home, they'd thrown them out when they moved from the place on Cow Creek. Just like that.

Politics, I decided, wasn't for me. Neither was selling cars. We moved to Portland. I got into commercial real estate. Our little tykes became teenagers. Irene was a great mom. What an Irish slob I was; four children and I never changed a diaper. Sometimes, we'd head back over the Coast Range for vacations at the beach. Or camped along the Nehalem

River, where my kids picked blackberries from the same bushes I'd once picked from as a kid. Life was good. But just when I thought I had put everything behind me and thought I was home free, I'd turn and see the wave building over my shoulder.

I don't know how Irene took it, my waking up in the middle of the night with the nightmares. Going into my midwinter funks, thinking of guys who'd be missing yet another Christmas with their families. December. January. Hate those months. Cold and dark. I still shiver because of the Bulge. One more day there and I honestly think I would have gotten hypothermia. Like a lot of other guys in Easy Company, I tried to drink away the memories.

Years passed. One December, in the 1970s, I'd been drinking at the Legion Club. I wasn't roaring drunk, but feeling good, so I thought I'd call Joe Toye in Pennsylvania. I called information and said I wanted the number for "Joseph J. Toye, Pittston, Pennsylvania." She said no such person was listed. So I said, "Is there anyone named Toye in Pennsylvania who owes your telephone company money?" She did some checking, then said, yes, he lives in West Reading, not Pittston. I said, "Would you ring him? That's him." It was. When I called, he'd just stumbled in from the bar. He was juiced and I was half-juiced. It was funny. But as time rolled on, it got so it wasn't funny anymore.

A few years later, living in Portland, I'd swing by some bar after work for a drink. There wasn't a glass of Scotch I brought to my lips that I wasn't back in Bastogne, where we were surrounded for eight straight days. Every time. One night, I was about sixty years old, I don't know what came over me. It was December. My job felt like a dead end. I was depressed. Before I knew it, I'd left a bar out on the east side and was headed east on Highway 26, toward Mount Hood. I knew of a curve flanked by a thousand-foot canyon. That was my target.

The car was swerving. It was snowing. Though not totally juiced, I had no business driving. As I climbed higher into the mountains, snow started lining the road, piled up by the plows. In my fogged-up mind, like the time I was standing around the campfire in Jack's Woods with that pistol in my hand, I'd somehow concocted this plan to end it all, just fly off a cliff and say to hell with it. Bury myself in that snowy canyon just like Skip had been buried in that snowy foxhole.

But when I reached the top of the pass, the image of Irene came into my mind. I pulled over to the side of the road and said to myself, *No. Not back in Bastogne. Not now. Not ever. This Malarkey doesn't quit.*

EPILOGUE
REMEMBERING THE BAND OF BROTHERS

At twenty-one, jumping out of airplanes and running Mount Currahee, you never stop to think you'll someday be eighty-six. But now I am. Unlike the time at Bastogne, where every minute seemed to take an hour, life now passes fast. One day you're taking on Hitler's army, the next day calling to cancel the newspaper because the kid can't get the blasted thing on the porch. One day you're jumping out of an airplane at more than one hundred miles per hour, the next day shuffling into the Cue Ball for three-cushion billiards every Thursday. Our battles change. But such is life. And despite the disappointments and pain, I wouldn't trade mine for anything.

My father died in 1955 of leukemia, my mother ten years

later of internal hemorrhaging. By then, I'd long gotten over their throwing out my stamp albums from Germany and the letters I'd sent home, and most of the other hurt as well.

Bernice Franetovich went on to become the singer she hoped to be. At age twenty-nine, she married a big-band musician and they had a great life together. Travel, skiing, bicycling across the country, the works. I got a letter from her a few years ago; her husband had passed away. She told me she was proud of how I'd served our country.

I did finally meet Faye Tanner, though, I'm ashamed to say, it wasn't me coming to see her like it should have been, but she coming to see me. She fell in love with a good man, a man who never insisted that she forget about Skip Muck. They were married in 1950. She kept Skip's wings, his eagle patch, the letters I sent her. When Stephen Ambrose's *Band of Brothers* and the HBO television series came out, she wound up being interviewed. A friend of mine saw her name in the paper and encouraged me to get in touch with her. It was hard—I'd let her down by not going to see her—but she was warm, gracious, and forgiving, just like the sweet woman I'd always imagined she would be. She sent me two letters that I'd sent her after Skip had died; she'd saved them all this time. In the nineties, she showed up at an Easy Company reunion at Fort Campbell in Kentucky. I put my arm around her and we both broke down and cried, meaning I'd cried with, or for, nearly everybody connected to the Easy Company story except for one person.

Our house on Kensington where I'd jumped off the roof with the beach umbrella is still there. The cabins on the Nehalem are long gone, and the Sigma Nu house at the

University of Oregon is where they filmed some fraternity scenes for that crazy movie *Animal House* back in the seventies.

Things change. I've changed. For the better I hope, though with me, it's always been one of those two-steps-foward-one-step-backward deals. After that night near Mount Hood, I cut back my drinking—and quit smoking. What got me on track was a handful of people: the love of my wife, Irene, and my family. And the guys of Easy Company. In 1978, I—a self-proclaimed Oregon hermit—met with two of our guys. The next year, I wrote to Dick Winters:

> *I don't think a day has passed in my life that I haven't thought about you and all the fine persons we were fortunate to serve with. Until a year and a half ago, I had very little contact with anyone from the company. I let Guarnere talk me into driving back to Missoula to meet with him and John Martin. Although Martin lives in Phoenix, he has a luxury summer home in Missoula. I am an Oregon hermit so that was quite a concession for me. There are not too many of us out this way. Tom Burgess lives in Vancouver, Washington and Rod Bain in Alaska. We have seen each other quite a bit. Jim Alley lives in Seattle. I have heard from Bob Rader, Joe Hogan, Welsh, Ranney, and Buck.*

In 1980, I went to Nashville for my first-ever Easy Company reunion; it was the first time my wife, Irene, and I had ever flown in a jet. (Ironically, a few decades after the war, I discovered why I froze up while in that orchard tree back in Normandy; I have acrophobia, a fear of heights, not common among paratroopers. The only way I could fly in my later years was to order a Scotch whiskey when

I got aboard and tell the flight attendant to keep 'em coming.)

At the Nashville reunion, I started realizing all the stuff I'd bottled up in me over the decades. On the first night of the reunion, a bunch of us—Joe Toye, Don Moone, Chuck Grant, Walter Gordon, and our wives—went to a club. My emotions from being back with these guys went nuts; I hadn't seen them in thirty-five years. I walked out of the club without Irene and headed back to the hotel. I got lost. Scared. Disoriented. The works. By the time I found myself back at the hotel, the lobby was full of Easy Company men who'd gotten so worried they'd sent the police after me. I guess I'd been in some pretty dangerous neighborhoods and hadn't known it. I felt like I'd let everyone down. Back home, I wrote most of the men with deep apologies. I also started realizing that maybe it wasn't such a bad idea to face some of this stuff inside that was making me crazy at times. Another letter to Winters:

> The reunion, in some respects, was overwhelming to me and an emotional experience that makes it difficult to collect one's thoughts in an orderly manner. Nevertheless, I shall remember with special significance my first reunion, even though it incorporated a traumatic event on my part. Irene was very reluctant about going to Nashville but after four days exposure to the men and traditions of the 101st Airborne she now considers it to be one of the most important happenings of our life.

It was freeing, I realized, to face the long-buried stuff. As I told Winters:

> Back in 1944–45, a person had to discipline his emotions to such an extent, in order to keep your head screwed on, that you

may not have properly demonstrated proper appreciation, compassion, sorrow, and the whole gamut of feelings that were rampant within you. I wanted you to know how grateful I was for your consideration of me throughout our entire time overseas. There was more than one instance when you very well may have saved my life—D-Day is one; ordering me in from the outpost in Holland, at Hell's Corner, when I was caught in a heavy mortar attack; and pulling me off a combat patrol in Haguenau are a few. I am sure there are more. . . . There has hardly been an hour pass since I left France in November 1945 that I have not thought of you and the tremendous officers and men of our company and the 101st Airborne. . . . It was without question the proudest and most cherished period of my life, even though there are times when I succumb to depths of sadness that I am not strong enough to withstand, when I dwell too much on memories of the men we left behind. I am not ashamed of it—the Irish are known to have emotional weaknesses and I am no exception—except I did stay in control in combat.

That, I've come to believe, is the hardest thing about war: to be faced with so many emotional situations involving people who've come to mean the world to you. Losing those people, sometimes right in front of you. And yet not being able to grieve for them. Even after the war, when you were expected to just get on with your life as if nothing more had happened to you than, say, a reshuffling of your living room furniture. I had a fraternity brother who contacted me when all the *Band of Brothers* stuff started coming out in the press. He said, "How in the hell could I have lived with you for four years and never known this stuff?" Because we keep it inside. In my whole life, I've never been to a counselor, even though I probably should have. As I wrote to Winters in 1980:

> *Perhaps the event that remains most vivid in my mind was when Skip Muck was killed. Medic Roe came to my foxhole to tell me about it and to ask me if I wanted to see Skip before he removed his body. I refused. Later, he returned and said that you suggested that I come back with you for a couple of days. I also refused to do that, knowing we were going back to Foy soon. The thoughtfulness you extended to me was appreciated far more than I tolerated myself to express back in those days.*

When Stephen Ambrose's book *Band of Brothers* came out in 1992, followed by the HBO miniseries almost a decade later, it was good for me. Not because of the attention; I didn't need that, though I've enjoyed speaking from time to time to various organizations around the world about my experiences and about leadership. But because it somehow reminded me that what we did was a good thing—and over the years I'd forgotten that. I remember getting a letter from Winters in 2003. "Who would have thought our stories would have been shared with the whole world?" he wrote. "We are indeed fortunate and have been blessed."

Still, that movie was an emotional roller coaster for me. I was called in as a consultant on some scenes, and it was tough. It brought everything back, especially later on when we all got to go to France for the premiere. Skip's family was there. What's so interesting is that the actor who I became closest with was Richard Speight Jr., the guy who played Skip in the miniseries. The first time he called me, he was politely asking me questions about Skip so he could better portray him, and damned if I didn't hang up on him. Not because he'd done or said anything wrong. Because I just couldn't take it.

But as the filming began and we got to know each other, Richard became a great support to me, this kid half a century younger than me. Never made me feel like some sentimental old fool. Told me he understood my emotions. Said it was OK, that I was emotional because Skip and I had meant so much to each other and that was a good thing, not a bad thing. That meant the world to me. You have to understand that it took me nearly forty years before I could look at our 1942 company picture and not break into tears, particularly if it was December or January.

I didn't like everything about the book or the movie. I wish Ambrose had included a handful of guys he ignored, instead of dwelling so much on a bit player like David Kenyon Webster. And the movie had a bit too much "Hollywood" in it for my taste. Nobody I've talked to from Easy Company remembers being at that Jewish concentration camp at Landsberg. The Carentan and Eindhoven fights—they made those out to be a helluva lot more than they were. That said, both the book and miniseries did what they set out to do—tell the story of this "band of brothers," most of it as it happened. And allowed me to talk about stuff that I hadn't talked about. And spend more time with the guys of Easy Company, though they're dwindling fast. At Toccoa, we'd had about 150 men. In 1984, we had forty-three men at the annual reunion; in 2002, the last one I attended, in Phoenix, we had thirty—and four actors from HBO's *Band of Brothers,* which meant the world to us. It's interesting, looking back at one of the photographs taken that weekend: There's Richard Speight Jr. (Skip), Scott Grimes (me), Michael Cudlitz (Denver "Bull" Randleman), and Matthew

Settle (Ronald Speirs). And who does Grimes, who played me, have his arm around? Richard Speight Jr., of course. The guy who played Skip.

In many ways, the Band of Brothers became like this large, extended family; we had trained together, suffered together, fought together, died together. Not that we always got along, before or after the war. I remember once, at a reunion in Dallas, Lewis Nixon and Harry Welsh and Mike Ranney sitting around, and Nixon tees off on Buck Compton. Says he was a coward. I said, "Is that right? And how many Silver Stars do *you* have?" They didn't know Buck Compton. They hadn't served with him as I had. Hadn't seen him rush those 105s at Brecourt Manor. Compton had been wounded in Holland, and was a damn good officer, a tough soldier, a guy who gave until he couldn't give anymore. Not a cowardly bone in his body.

Usually, we got along much better. The Muck and Penkala families—Skip and Alex died together in Bastogne—became extremely close friends and remain so today. In the mideighties, Winters got no less than forty-one Christmas cards from Easy Company guys—forty years after the war was over. I remember getting a letter from Harry Welsh, back in 1979, thanking me for volunteering to take that patrol by myself into that factory along the Rhine River, where the kid named Orth took a ricocheted bullet in the knee. For many, the reunions were among the highlights of our older years. But like all families, the Band of Brothers have experienced their pain.

It's sad looking back at some of the letters I sent Winters over the years: "I do not see how Burr Smith can make it much longer. . . . I have had dozens of my friends and relatives from WWII who drank themselves to death. . . . I was sorry to hear about Mike Ranney." Ranney, one of the guys who'd triggered the ouster of Sobel, wound up living in a boarding house in Reno and was found all by himself, dying. Years before, he'd brought a written apology to the guys at a reunion for being out of position and getting shot at Brecourt Manor in Normandy.

At one reunion, I got on an elevator and there was a guy wearing these dirty old clothes and smelling of booze. A severe alcoholic. Not until later did I realize it was a Toccoa guy. Don Moone and Walter Gordon took him to a room, stripped his clothes off, and got him everything new with more to take with him. It was sad.

Joe Toye, unable to work in the mines, spent his whole life sharpening giant drill bits for a coal-mining operation. One year, a few of us cooked up a deal to get Joe and his wife, Betty, some free airline tickets so they could come to a reunion. He died in 1995. I called the night before he died and thanked him for all he'd done for me. Later, I got a letter from his son, Pete. He was then working in the athletic department at the University of Wyoming. Joe had had a tough life. He and this kid's mother had divorced; Joe and his boy had a tough go of it.

So I wrote Pete a letter and told him about the Joe Toye I'd known in Bastogne and the hell his father had been through and how he'd saved my life when Dewitt Lowery had threatened to stick that knife in my gut. He framed that letter, stuck it on his wall, and wrote back:

This has been a very emotional day for me ever since I received your letter. I'm half Irish and that half can get me blub-

bering easily even without a few beers. My father was a hard man. As hard as the Anthracite he shoveled in his youth and the drill bits he sharpened later in life at Grace Mines. He was not a touchy-feely guy and I think he harbored a lot of emotional pain and frustration from the war. That pain and frustration was most obvious when he drank but, as I get older, I understand him more and more. With reading the books of Company E exploits and seeing Saving Private Ryan *I am now getting a much clearer picture of what being trained as elite warriors entailed and how death and dismemberment and the associated psychological trauma you all dealt with must have affected your postwar lives. For my dad, I believe he fought those ghosts the best he could in a time when real men dealt with their own baggage and never whined or cried or appeared weak. He was my rock against which I have measured my responses to my own life struggles.*

In hindsight, I suppose, my father had some ghosts of his own. No, he hadn't fought in a war. But he'd lost two brothers to war. And lost a business. A house. His pride. In a way, his family. Strange, isn't it? As with Pete Toye, we don't start figuring out the old man until after he's gone.

Lots of good things spun off from all the *Band of Brothers* attention. The movie *Saving Private Ryan* came out of Ambrose's book after Tom Hanks read about the Niland brothers. I'd told Ambrose the story about Skip and me having drinks with the Niland brothers in London. They'd known Skip because they'd grown up in upstate New York where he had. I told Ambrose how, after D-day, Fritz Niland showed up near Carentan, looking for Skip. One of his brothers had been killed, he said. Turned out three of them had been killed. So he was immediately tracked down, though not by an army platoon as in *Saving Private Ryan,* but by a Catholic chaplain, and shipped home. "Don Malarkey's story in *Band of Brothers* about going to London . . . and visiting the Niland brothers . . . is the story behind the story of the movie, *Saving Private Ryan,*" Dick Winters has asserted in writing.

Because of the *Band of Brothers* attention, I've taken trips everywhere. Lots of fun. Lots of memories. The other day I was at Wal-Mart and had on an Easy Company jacket, and this kid comes up to me as we're getting our shopping carts and says, "You're . . . you're . . ."

"Don Malarkey," I said. "Now you'd better take care of your shopping cart, son."

The attention has been nice. It's nice to know you haven't been forgotten and to think somehow you left a mark on the world. Some people live their whole lives and can never really say they did anything for humanity. We did and can. But for all the attention, the darker side of war follows you. The wave is always there, building behind you, never going away. Ever since the march to Atlanta, I've had trouble walking at a quick pace or running. I get cold in December, even though Oregon rarely gets below thirty-five degrees. And I remember the guys we left behind. Every day, I remember.

But once, while walking the beach near Astoria, I saw these birds—puffins, I think—floating amid these giant waves that were about to break on them. And they did the damnedest thing: Knowing they couldn't ignore those waves or outswim them, they turned and faced the swells head-on, dove right into them, realizing they'd be safer that way.

It was a good lesson for me.

Irene died in the spring of 2006 after a bout with breast cancer. We'd been married nearly sixty years, which is a long time, longer if you're married to me. What a woman. People admired me for what I'd done, but they admired her for who she was. I think of a line from that crazy Engelbert Humperdinck song: "Thanks for taking me on a one-way trip to the sun." I didn't deserve someone so refined and dignified. Now, when I give my homemade jam to friends, every label says the same thing: "Oregon's Wild Blackberries: Picked & Processed by Don Malarkey in Loving Memory of His Wife Irene."

The year after she died was hell, especially Christmastime. But we'd had some great times. In the last twenty-five years, we'd gone to a lot of Easy Company reunions. She never begrudged me that stuff. Our house was—still is—filled with books and photos and posters about Easy Company; it's just a helluva lot dirtier now that she's not around. And lonelier. There's a certain nobility, as the poem "Invictus" suggests, in being the "captain of your soul." But when you're alone, that me-against-the-world stuff isn't all it's cracked up to be.

We had gone to Europe a handful of times, Irene and I, to see many of the places where Easy Company had been decades ago. Enough to fill eighty albums with photos. We spent an afternoon with Michel de Vallavielle, who had been twenty-four when we'd fought the Germans on his family's farm, Brecourt Manor, in Normandy, and had accidentally been shot by one of our guys. He showed us the stains on the floor where two German officers had died four decades before—at the hands of Easy Company. And bites out of a rock wall, courtesy of my mortar firing. In 1984, we went to Charing Cross Road where the Palace Pub had once stood, where I'd spent so many afternoons shooting the bull with Pat McGrath. It was now some sort of fast-food restaurant.

We walked along the dikes of Hell's Corner in Holland. In Eindhoven, in 2006, we were being honored—Dick Winters was being named an honorary citizen—and they had the British singer Vera Lynn singing the song she'd debuted in 1939, "We'll Meet Again."

We'll meet again, don't know where, don't know when . . .

She hadn't sung more than three words when I collapsed into an emotional heap. Bill Guarnere and Babe Heffron had to hold me up. Supposedly it was the last time she ever sang that song.

The first time I saw Skip Muck's grave at the Luxembourg American Cemetery and Memorial, I just stood there and felt numb. I was with Dick Winters and Carwood Lipton, on a trip led by Stephen Ambrose. It was 1991. No tears. In fact, there's a photo of three of us old vets standing at his grave and we're all looking resolute. Soldiers, you know, posing for a picture taken by a historian who admired the hell out of us.

I returned there in 2004 and remembered how when Roe asked if I wanted to see Skip, I'd said no. And when Winters asked if I wanted a break, I'd said no. I realized that since those moments, I'd grieved for everybody I'd lost except for one man, the man whose death I'd tried for decades to run away from, the man whose loss had hit me harder than all the rest.

How many times had I looked at that 1942 photo of all of us at Toccoa, the one I'd written all the KIAs and SWAs on for those killed and seriously wounded, and thought, Why not me? Why no initials on *my* chest? Why not at Brecourt Manor, when I'd stupidly gone after what I thought was a Luger on that dead soldier? Or at Hell's Corner, when German soldiers had our patrol outnumbered eight to three but wrongly assumed we had more firepower and surrendered to us? Or at Bastogne? If Winters hadn't split Skip and me up, that would probably have been me, not Penkala, in that foxhole with Skip on January 9, 1944.

But even if I've played the what-if game often, I know, deep down, that you can never win at it. Better to remember that, for whatever reason—God or fate or reading a *Reader's Digest* article about paratroopers on a Greyhound bus heading for Astoria—I was privileged to serve with a company of men who would make me far more than I would have been without them. And that losing one of those men had hurt so badly that I'd buried the thought of him, thinking that somehow that would help me avoid the pain.

Better, I've since learned, to turn into those waves and dive. So on that day in 2004 when I visited the cemetery where Skip is buried, I looked at that white marble cross and that name—Sgt. Warren H. Muck—and thought of the kid who swam the Niagara. The march to Atlanta. The smile. I knelt, placed flowers at the base of that cross. Prayed. All the things I'd done before when I'd come to see his grave. Only this time I did something different, long overdue, and hard but freeing.

I cried sixty years' worth of tears.

AFTERWORD

After the HBO *Band of Brothers* series premiered in 2001, I began receiving invitations to speak at various business and educational meetings. On one occasion, a police academy training conference asked me to present my experiences in a leadership-training format. I was a bit taken aback, but thought it could be done. I contacted Vance Day, a good friend of mine and a local attorney, who had worked as a history teacher. I figured that he was familiar with putting together something along the lines of what the conference wanted. I was right. Vance jumped right into it and we created an ever-evolving presentation called *Frontline Leadership*.

We presented it first at the police academy conference, and we began getting calls from other police, firefighter, and military organizations. *Frontline Leadership* was adapted into various formats to fit different needs: after-dinner presentation, ninety-minute, four-hour, and eight-hour versions. Vance put together a course syllabus for those organizations needing class credit. Pretty soon we were giving the presentation three to four times a month. It was kind of a "Mutt and Jeff" show. Vance would run video clips and give the leadership theory side of the presentation. I would share stories from my Easy Company and life experiences that exemplified the points we were making. The two of us have a great deal of fun together, and the audiences enjoy it.

Since that initial event we have given the presentation, in one form or another, dozens of times. Vance and I have traveled Europe and North America together, lectured at the United States Military Academy at West Point, the Lazard Lecture Series, Focus on the Family's National Family Policy Conference, the Heritage Foundation, the Family Research Council, in addition to various military bases and numerous organizations and educational institutions. Not a bad run. In May of 2005 we were asked to give *Frontline Leadership* on Capitol Hill for members of Congress, followed by a presentation to senior staff at the White House. Buck Compton joined us for Washington, D.C., events and on several other occasions. Bill Guarnere even joined on a trip to New York City to give a presentation.

I feel humbled by the attention, even a bit embarrassed. But then I remember that I owe it to the guys who did not return. It's as if I am keeping faith with them. Somehow, as I tell of their courage, trauma, and accomplishments, I am helping to establish a legacy of leadership for future generations. So many Americans have done so much that we might enjoy this liberty that we, and other nations, possess. *Front-*

line Leadership brings home that point. It reminds people that we have such a rich heritage of sacrifice that not only demands our reverence, but calls us to leave a legacy. We are Americans—we lead and are looked to as leaders in the fight for liberty. We dare not shirk this responsibility.

ACKNOWLEDGMENTS

Don Malarkey:

Thanks to the following people for helping me tell my story: Col. Mike Poell, Col. Terry Williams, James Lebold, Dale Shank, Jerry Sullivan, Leonard Tong, Jane Wiles, Bernice Franetovich DuLong (whose stage name was Bernice Franette), Terry Muir, Paul Isley, Tamil Edsall, Bill Van Dusen, Henry Yoshiki, Dan McNally, Tim Serean, John Hill, Tom Hill, Neil Everett Morfit, Lisa Penner, Sharon Keudell, Dr. David and Mary Kay Foster, and last, but not least, to all my grandchildren and great-grandchildren.

A special thanks to one of my truest and closest friends, Vance Day. Although half my age, he is like a brother to me, always encouraging, stretching, and challenging me. He's helped me to work through the pain I've buried since the war. Without Vance's tenacious prodding, this book would not have been written.

Without the dedication and hard work of Greg Johnson, my book agent, this project would never have become reality. Greg and staff at Wordserve Literary believed in the book from the beginning and worked hard to bring it to you, the reader. Thank you Greg.

Bob Welch:

Thanks to those who edited the original manuscript: Ann Petersen, Ron Palmer, Pat Gariepy, and Sally Welch. To those who put pieces into the puzzle of who Don is: his daughters, Marianne McNally, Martha Serean, and Sharon Hill; Rod Bain, who served with Don in Easy Company; Pete Toye, son of Joe Toye; Eileen O'Hara, niece of Skip Muck; Bernice Franetovich DuLong, Don's former girlfriend; and Richard Speight Jr., who played Skip Muck in the HBO miniseries, *Band of Brothers*. To Don's son, Michael, for his assistance. To Vance Day, who not only helped edit, but served as a wonderful liaison between Don and me. And, finally, to Don himself, who began this project as my subject but wound up as my friend and a man I admire greatly.

INDEX